C000160575

English Skills 3

Answers

Carol Matchett

Schofield & Sims

Which book?

The **English Skills** books are aligned with the end-of-year objectives for Key Stage 2. For the majority of pupils aged seven to 11 years, follow the guidance given on page 2 as to which book to use with each year group.

If a pupil is working significantly above or below the standard normally expected for his or her age, another book may be more appropriate. If you are not sure which to choose, **Workbook descriptors** and a simple **Entry test** are available to help you identify the book that is best suited to the pupil's abilities. You can also use these resources with new pupils joining your class or school.

Photocopy masters of the **Workbook descriptors** and **Entry test** are provided in the **Teacher's Guide** – which also contains the **Entry test marking key**, full instructions for use, and a range of other **English Skills** copymasters. For ordering details, see page 46.

You may be using **English Skills** at Key Stage 3 or with other mixed-ability groups of young people or adults. In such cases you will find the **Workbook descriptors** and **Entry test** vital in deciding which book to give each student.

Published by Schofield & Sims Ltd,
Dogley Mill, Fenay Bridge, Huddersfield HD8 0NQ, UK
Telephone 01484 607080

www.schofieldandsims.co.uk

Copyright © Schofield and Sims Ltd, 2011

Author: Carol Matchett
Carol Matchett has asserted her moral right under the Copyright, Designs and Patents Act, 1988, to be identified as the author of this work.

***British Library** Cataloguing in Publication Data*
A catalogue record for this book is available from the British Library.

All rights reserved. Except where otherwise indicated, no part of this publication may be reproduced, stored in a retrieval system, or transmitted in any form or by any means, electronic, mechanical, photocopying, recording or otherwise, without either the prior permission of the publisher or a licence permitting restricted copying in the United Kingdom issued by the Copyright Licensing Agency Limited, Saffron House, 6–10 Kirby Street, London WC1N 8TS.

*The **Writing task assessment sheets** (pages 16, 30 and 44) and the **Completed proofreading tasks** (pages 17, 31 and 45) are exempt from these restrictions and may be photocopied for use within the purchaser's institution only.*

Commissioning and editorial project management by
***Carolyn Richardson Publishing Services** (www.publiserve.co.uk)*

*Design by **Ledgard Jepson Ltd***
*Printed in the UK by **Wyndeham Gait Ltd**, Grimsby, Lincolnshire*

Book 3 Answers ISBN 978 07217 1183 6

Contents

Schofield & Sims English Skills 3 Answers

SECTION 1

Spelling: Rules for plural spelling and verb endings. Irregular tense changes. Shortened forms with apostrophes. Words with double consonants.

Word structure: Adding prefixes and suffixes to create new words; changing word class; rules for adding vowel suffixes. Synonyms.

Vocabulary: Homographs and homophones in context. Improving verb choice. Writing definitions; using context and word structure to infer meaning. Collecting and classifying words.

Sentence structure: Subordinating conjunctions; connectives to link sentences; combining information; adding phrases. Using adverbs. Editing.

Punctuation: Sentence punctuation; punctuating dialogue and quotations. Commas to demarcate meaningful units, adverbs and extra information.

Grammar: Checking agreement. Past and future tense. Using powerful verbs for effect; selecting appropriate adverbs, adjectives.

SECTION 2

Spelling: Spelling rules for adding prefixes and suffixes; common word endings and patterns. Checking spellings.

Word structure: Adding prefixes (**al**, **a**, **ad**); suffixes to change class of word. Forming comparatives and superlatives. Root words.

Vocabulary: Alternatives to common words; synonyms and antonyms. Words with more than one meaning. Archaic words. Scales of intensity.

Sentence structure: Moving adverbs and phrases. Adding clauses to explain. Extending sentences. Editing. Rewriting notes as full sentences. Similes.

Punctuation: Commas to separate clauses. Apostrophes for contraction and possession.

Grammar: Writing adjectival phrases. Impact of adverbs on meaning. Using comparatives and superlatives. Powerful, expressive verbs to create moods.

SECTION 3

Spelling: Common letter strings with different pronunciations. Spelling of common homophones. Spelling rules and exceptions. Spelling strategies.

Word structure: Adding suffixes (**tion**, **ive**, **ist**, **ible/able**). Compound words (including some with hyphens). Meaning of common roots.

Vocabulary: Using word structures and origins to infer meaning.

Sentence structure: Changing sentence types (statement, order, question). Using adverbs, phrases, clauses to clarify/emphasise point of view.

Punctuation: Apostrophe for possession (plurals). More complex punctuation (colon, dash, semi-colon, hyphen).

Grammar: Choosing words for impact; figurative and expressive language. Word classes.

Teacher's notes

Introduction to the series

Schofield & Sims English Skills provides regular and carefully graded practice in key literacy skills. It is designed for use alongside your existing literacy lessons, embedding key aspects of grammar, sentence structure, punctuation and spelling and constantly revisiting them until they become automatic. At the same time it reinforces and develops pupils' knowledge of word structure and vocabulary.

Each workbook comprises three sections with 12 tests in each one. The tests become more difficult, but the increase in difficulty is gradual. The workbooks are fully compatible with the Key Stage 2 literacy curriculum and the final tests in each book are aligned with the end-of-year objectives as follows:

- **Book 1:** Year 2
- **Book 2:** Year 3
- **Book 3:** Year 4
- **Book 4:** Year 5
- **Book 5:** Year 6
- **Book 6:** Years 6/7

Please note: Pupils working towards the objectives for an earlier year should use the appropriate workbook. There is no need for all members of the class to be working on the same book at the same time.

Parts A, B and C

Each test is divided into three parts:

- Part A: **Warm-up** – puzzles, 'warm-up' exercises and revision of earlier learning
- Part B: **Word work** – spelling, word structure, exploring words and their meanings
- Part C: **Sentence work** – putting words together to make sentences: for example, choosing suitable words, forming and punctuating sentences or checking for grammatical accuracy.

Answering the test questions

After you have demonstrated to the class how some of the different question types are to be answered, the pupils work through the test items without adult help – either individually or in pairs. For Books 2 to 6, encourage them to refer to dictionaries, thesauruses and other reference materials rather than asking for your help. The tests may be used flexibly. For example, a test may be tackled in one session or over several days.

Marking

This book provides correct answers for **English Skills 3**; where various different answers would be acceptable, an example is provided. The **Focus** panel stating the areas of learning being tested helps you to decide whether the pupil's answer is satisfactory. **Please note and explain to the class that if all or part of a question has several possible answers, the question number is displayed like this 5 . If a question has a specific answer, the question number is displayed like this 5 . It is displayed in this way even if the answer is made up of several parts that may be given in any order.**

Some questions test more than one area: for example, a question on writing in the past tense might also check pupils' knowledge of the spelling rules for adding **ed**. In such cases, both parts of the answer must be correct, reflecting real-life situations that require varied knowledge and skills.

Group marking sessions

Group or class marking sessions led by the teacher or classroom assistant are the most effective way of marking the tests: pupils learn by comparing and discussing answers.

Another benefit of group or class marking sessions is that they highlight deficits in pupils' knowledge, which will inform your future teaching. Where pupils have given a wrong answer, or none at all, briefly reinforce the key teaching point using an item from this book as a model. In a plenary discussion at the end of the session, encourage pupils to evaluate their own successes; each pupil can then work with a 'talk partner' to record areas needing improvement and discuss appropriate learning objectives.

Suggested questions to ask in a marking session:

- How many different 'correct' answers did we come up with?
- Were some sentence or word choices more interesting or effective than others? Why?
- How do you know this answer is correct?
- How can we make the answer correct?
- Is there an answer that would be even better?
- What are the success criteria for this type of question?
- What are the key points to remember next time?
- When might we put these key points into practice in our reading or writing?

Marking the end-of-section assessments

At the end of each workbook section are two writing assessments: the independent writing task and the proofreading task. These check that pupils are applying in their writing the knowledge, skills and understanding developed in the weekly tests. The assessments also provide evidence of a pupil's strengths and weaknesses, which will help you to set appropriate targets. You might consider sharing with the pupils a simplified version of the mark scheme – and then involve them in setting their own targets, as discussed above.

- ***The independent writing task***

The independent writing task gives you a snapshot of a pupil's writing development. Prompts help pupils to plan and gather ideas so that when they begin writing they can focus on expressing their ideas clearly and effectively. On pages 16, 30 and 44 you will find photocopiable **Writing task assessment sheets** – one for each section – with specific assessment points arranged under the headings 'Sentence structure and punctuation', 'Composition and effect' and 'Spelling'. Complete one of these sheets as you mark each pupil's work.

- ***The proofreading task***

The proofreading task focuses on punctuation, grammar and spelling. Examples of **Completed proofreading tasks** for each section, also photocopiable, are supplied on pages 17, 31 and 45. However, please note that pupils may choose to correct some of the errors using methods different to those shown in the example but equally valid. For example, two unpunctuated strings of words might be joined using a connective or separated to make two sentences. Additional evidence gained from the relevant proofreading task will help you to further assess pupils' achievements in 'Sentence punctuation' and 'Spelling' as already assessed in the writing task. If you wish, you can use the photocopiable sheet to make notes on a pupil's work.

Please note: Pupils whose scores against the assessment statements are low do not need to repeat a section. All the books revisit difficult areas and offer ample opportunities for further practice. Instead of holding a pupil back, highlight the assessment statements that reveal his or her weaknesses and use these to set learning targets. Ensure that pupils know their targets as they begin the next section.

Progress chart

On page 46 of the pupil workbook only you will find a **Progress chart**, with one column each for Sections 1, 2 and 3, and a list of 'I can' statements relating to the kinds of activities practised in the section. Please ask every pupil to complete the relevant column when they have finished working through a section.

The **Progress chart** encourages pupils to monitor their own work by identifying those activities that they have mastered and those requiring further attention. When pupils colour in the chart as recommended (**green** for **easy**, **orange** for **getting there** and **red** for **difficult**) it gives a clear picture of progress. It also shows the benefits of systematic practice: an activity that the pupil cannot perform in Section 1 later gets the 'green light'.

The **Progress chart** promotes assessment for learning and personalised learning. Whilst it is best completed in the workbook, so that achievements in all sections may be compared, you may at some point wish to have additional copies. For this reason, it may be photocopied. **However, all other pages of the pupil workbook remain strictly non-photocopiable.**

Section 1 Test 1

A WARM-UP

Cross out the nouns. Write new nouns that make the sentence different.

1 The ~~cat~~ watched the ~~bird~~ from behind the ~~tree~~.

| child | burglar | door |

2 The ~~librarian~~ put three ~~books~~ on the ~~shelf~~.

| baker | loaves | counter |

3 The ~~gardener~~ picked up the ~~plant~~ from the ~~garden~~.

| bus | people | village |

> **PART A Focus**
> **1–3:** choice of nouns
> **4–6:** spelling vowel phonemes
> **7–10:** synonyms

Write three words that rhyme.

4 **first** | burst | worst | thirst

5 **break** | wake | take | steak

6 **saw** | more | four | door

Write two synonyms.

7 **furious** | angry | annoyed

8 **foolish** | stupid | unwise

9 **brave** | bold | courageous

10 **sly** | crafty | cunning

B WORD WORK

1 Make the word plural.

| **delay** | delays | **city** | cities |
| **army** | armies | **journey** | journeys |

2 What spelling rule did you use?

If there is a vowel before the 'y', add 's'. If not change 'y' to 'i' and add 'es'.

Write a definition of the word in **bold**.

3 He looked at his **watch**.

watch: a device for telling the time

4 **Watch** carefully.

watch: look or observe

5 I am reading this **book**.

book: something you read

6 We must **book** a room for the party.

book: reserve, put your name down for

> **PART B Focus**
> **1–2:** plural spelling rules
> **3–6:** homonyms; meaning from context
> **7–10:** prefixes

Add the same prefix to all three words.

7 re turn | re play | re bound

8 mis fortune | mis hear | mis count

9 non -smoking | non -stop | non -drip

10 dis appoint | dis connect | dis own

C SENTENCE WORK

What punctuation mark is hidden by the symbol?

Boy: Help▼ Wolf♦ wolf▼   **Shepherd:** Where■ Where is the wolf■

Boy: Surprise▼ There is no wolf really.

1 ▼ is an exclamation mark (!)

2 ♦ is a comma (,)

3 ■ is a question mark (?)

> **PART C Focus**
> **1–3:** question marks, exclamation marks and commas
> **4–7:** precise choice of adjectives
> **8–10:** conjunctions; sentence variation

Cross out any adjectives that you think are unnecessary.

4 The ~~hot, shiny, brilliant~~ sun shone on the scorched earth.

5 A flashing light beamed from the ~~glass~~ window of the ~~tall~~ tower.

6 The children were dressed in ~~tatty, scruffy,~~ filthy rags.

7 The extra adjectives are unnecessary because they don't add anything new.

Write the sentence so it begins with the connective.

8 He stopped to rest **when** it grew dark.   When it grew dark he stopped to rest.

9 A hand grabbed him **as** he jumped.   As he jumped, a hand grabbed him.

10 He could not escape **although** he tried.   Although he tried to escape, he could not.

X DEFINITIVE ANSWER   X SAMPLE ANSWER

A WARM-UP

Write a sentence using these words.

1 **dark scream quiet**

It was just getting dark when a scream cut through the quiet evening.

2 **woke hungry bed**

I woke up feeling hungry and jumped out of bed.

Write an antonym.

PART A Focus
1–2: sentence formation
3–5: antonyms
6–7: plural spelling rules
8–10: question marks; exclamation marks

3 **possible** unlikely

4 **agreeable** unpleasant

5 **definite** uncertain

Write the nouns as plurals.

6 **daisy** daisies **rose** roses

7 **banana** bananas **peach** peaches

Put a question mark or an exclamation mark at the end of each headline.

8 'Tree-mendous' job !

9 Have you caught the walking bug ?

10 Sarah takes the plunge !

B WORD WORK

Complete the verb sums.

1 **carry** + ed = carried

2 **carry** + s = carries

3 **display** + ed = displayed

4 **display** + s = displays

PART B Focus
1–5: rules for adding ed and s
6–9: technical verbs; word meanings
10: prefixes

5 What spelling rule did you use?

Change the 'y' to an 'i' and add 'ed' or 'es'. If there is a vowel before the 'y', leave it as it is.

Write the verb beside the correct definition.

evaluate evacuate consider conserve

6 evacuate move from danger

7 conserve save or protect

8 consider think about

9 evaluate decide the value of

10 Draw a line to join the prefix and the root word.

sub ———— flow

pre ———— marine

contra ———— view

C SENTENCE WORK

Proofread the story. Add the missing punctuation and capital letters.

PART C Focus
1–3: punctuating sentence boundaries
4–6: powerful verbs
7–10: conjunctions; giving reasons

1 The car slowed down. It seemed to be following someone. Who was it?

2 An hour passed. No-one came. It was getting dark.

3 Jed turned off his torch. The rain poured down. What now?

Cross out the verb **went**. Write a new verb that makes the character sound angry.

4 The man ~~went~~ out of the room. charged

5 The Prince ~~went~~ out of the palace. stormed

6 Michelle ~~went~~ off. stomped

Continue the sentence to explain or give a reason.

7 You cannot see a dinosaur now because they have all died out.

8 A yacht moves quickly when there is a strong wind.

9 Doctors look at X-rays so that they can see if any bones are broken.

10 The after-school club will have to close if it cannot find more helpers.

X DEFINITIVE ANSWER   X SAMPLE ANSWER

Section 1   Test 3

A   WARM-UP

Write the next sentence.

1   Jack sat down and rested under a tree.

Suddenly, *a wolf sprang out.*

2   Jack sat down and rested under a tree.

Meanwhile, *Jill carried on digging.*

3   Jack sat down and rested under a tree.

Later, *Jill found him fast asleep.*

Draw a line to join the synonyms.

4   **finally** — at last

5   **suddenly** — all of a sudden

6   **meanwhile** — at the same time

7   **soon** — before long

Complete the word chain.

> PART A Focus
> 1–3: linked sentences; connectives
> 4–7: synonyms
> 8–10: rules for adding er and est

cold   colder   coldest

8   soft   *softer*   *softest*

9   close   *closer*   *closest*

10   hot   *hotter*   *hottest*

B   WORD WORK

Write the word with an apostrophe added.

1   **Im**   *I'm*   **couldnt**   *couldn't*

2   **cant**   *can't*   **didnt**   *didn't*

Add the verb endings.   **s   ing**

3   **touch**   *touches*   *touching*

4   **dash**   *dashes*   *dashing*

5   **buzz**   *buzzes*   *buzzing*

> PART B Focus
> 1–2: apostrophes in short forms
> 3–5: rules for adding s and ing
> 6–7: suffixes
> 8–10: homonyms; homographs

The words and suffixes are mixed up. Write them correctly.

6   run**less**   fashion**ly**   real**able**   speech**y**

runny   *fashionable*   *really*   *speechless*

7   punish**hood**   foolish**ment**   child**ness**

punishment   *foolishness*   *childhood*

Write a definition of the word in **bold**.

8   He took a **bow** at the end of the play.

A bow is *a bend forwards at the waist.*

9   We tied the ribbon in a **bow**.

A bow is *a fancy knot.*

10   He had a **bow** and arrow.

A bow is *a weapon that shoots arrows.*

C   SENTENCE WORK

Add the punctuation and capital letters to the dialogue.

1   "Are we nearly there?" asked ~~j~~**J**enny.

2   "That's the third time you've asked," sighed Dad. "~~t~~**T**ry to be patient."

3   "But I'm bored," grumbled ~~j~~**J**enny.

> PART C Focus
> 1–3: punctuating dialogue; apostrophes in short forms
> 4–6: precise word choice for effect
> 7–10: sentence structure; phrases to clarify **where**

Cross out three words. Write three new words to create a different picture.

4   The ~~car sped~~ down the ~~motorway.~~   horse   trotted   lane

5   The ~~street~~ was full of ~~shoppers~~ with brightly coloured ~~bags.~~   circus   acrobats   costumes

6   A ~~mouse scampered~~ from the ~~hole.~~   caveman   emerged   cave

Continue the sentence to say **what happened** and **where**.

7   Last night, a young child *was rescued from a fire at his home in Hyde.*

8   On Saturday, a car *crashed into a bus on the high street.*

9   Many years ago, an old man *found a wooden box in his garden.*

10   One summer's evening, Nina *was taking a walk in the village.*

| X DEFINITIVE ANSWER   X SAMPLE ANSWER |

Section 1   Test 4

A   WARM-UP

Finish the sentence.

1 Alfie was in a good mood because
his team had won.

2 Alfie was in a good mood until
he saw the state of his garden.

3 Alfie was in a good mood so
he bought us ice-creams.

Write the pairs of words that rhyme.
Add two more words to each pair.

**stood most score third
drawer could coast heard**

PART A Focus
1–3: using conjunctions
4–7: alternative spellings of vowel phonemes
8–10: soft c sound

4	stood	could	would	hood
5	most	coast	boast	host
6	score	drawer	more	for
7	third	heard	bird	word

8 What do the words have in common?

cinema circus city
They all start with a soft 'c'.

Write two more words that are similar.

9 _circle_   **10** _citizen_

B   WORD WORK

Cross out the words that are wrongly spelt.
Write the correct spellings.

1 As ~~thay warkt~~ it ~~bigan~~ to ~~raine.~~
they   _walked_   _began_   _rain_

2 He ~~thort~~ for a ~~wile,~~ then ~~startid~~ to ~~rite.~~
thought   _while_   _started_   _write_

3 ~~Lets' leeve~~ on ~~tyme~~ for a ~~chainge.~~
Let's   _leave_   _time_   _change_

PART B Focus
1–3: common spelling errors
4–7: meaning of prefixes
8–10: synonyms for common verbs

4 The words all have the same prefix.
Underline it.

prefix preschool preview predict

5 What does it mean?   _before_

6 The words all have the same prefix. Underline it.

submarine subway subheading

7 What does it mean?   _under_

Write three synonyms for the verb.

8	**find**	locate	discover	uncover
9	**jump**	leap	spring	bound
10	**look**	glance	stare	gaze

C   SENTENCE WORK

Add the missing punctuation.

PART C Focus
1–4: full stops, question marks, exclamation marks, apostrophes
5–8: past tense; regular and irregular verbs
9–10: time, linking phrases

1 **Shopkeeper:** Can I help you?

2 **Leanne:** I hope so. I am looking for some magic dust.

3 **Shopkeeper:** Magic dust! What makes you think you'll get magic dust here?

4 **Leanne:** It's a long story.

Write the sentence in the past tense.

5 The police stop the speeding car. At six o'clock last night, _the police stopped the speeding car._

6 The pirates find buried treasure. Last year, _the pirates found buried treasure._

7 He will finally be leaving the club on Friday. Last Friday, _he finally left the club._

8 The author is writing a new story. Last year, _the author wrote a new story._

9 Write the phrases in order of time, starting with the smallest.

by daybreak, many years passed, the next moment, several weeks later

the next moment, by daybreak, several weeks later, many years passed

10 Write two phrases that could be used instead of **the next moment**.

just then   _at that very moment_

X DEFINITIVE ANSWER   X SAMPLE ANSWER

Section 1 Test 5

A WARM-UP

1 Write a sentence using these words.

man television explosion

The man was watching television when suddenly there was an explosion.

Underline the word that is **not** a real word.

2 sadness <u>joyness</u> wickedness

3 avoidable drinkable <u>fearable</u>

4 endless <u>wishless</u> nameless

> **PART A Focus**
> **1:** sentence composition
> **2–4:** suffixes
> **5–7:** clarifying reasons
> **8–10:** silent letters

Continue the sentence so that it gives a reason.

5 He began to sneeze _because someone had spilt pepper everywhere._

6 Mia screamed _as the alien came closer._

7 He climbed a tree _to find out if he could see the village._

Each word in the pair is missing the same silent letter. Write the words correctly.

8 **bom** _bomb_   **crum** _crumb_

9 **rapper** _wrapper_   **reck** _wreck_

10 **naw** _gnaw_   **nome** _gnome_

B WORD WORK

Add a prefix and/or a suffix to the word **like** to match the definition.

un ly ness able

1 _likeable_   pleasant and friendly

2 _likely_   very probably true

3 _likeness_   something looking similar

4 _unlikely_   doubtful

> **PART B Focus**
> **1–4:** prefixes; suffixes; word meanings
> **5–6:** word meanings
> **7–10:** apostrophes in short forms

Write a definition of the word in **bold**.

5 There was a **lavish** feast.

lavish: _plentiful, abundant_

6 Mr Martin was in a **genial** mood.

genial: _friendly_

Add the missing apostrophe. Then write the full form.

7 t h e y'd   _they would_ or _they had_

8 I'd   _I would_ or _I had_

9 w o n't   _will not_

10 y o u've   _you have_

C SENTENCE WORK

Rewrite the sentences so that they say **where** and **when**.

1 A car crashed into a bus shelter. _Today, a car crashed into a bus shelter in town._

2 Elford lost 3–0. _On Saturday, Elford Town lost 3–0 at Norton._

3 There was a fire. _There was a fire at the factory last night._

4 Thieves escaped with a million pounds.
On Monday, thieves escaped from the bank with a million pounds.

Underline the verbs.

5 Tara <u>paced</u> up and down, <u>fiddling</u> with her lucky charm.

6 Why were these verbs chosen? _To show that Tara was anxious._

Use the verb to write a sentence about a character.

7 **glanced**   _Ben glanced over his shoulder._

8 **peered**   _Sal peered through the window._

9 **shuddered**   _Ally shuddered at the thought._

10 Proofread the poem. Add the missing punctuation and capital letters.
On Monday Zac felt great, on Tuesday he felt blue.
Today Zac is feeling fine, so how are things with you?

> **PART C Focus**
> **1–4:** adding phrases to clarify meaning
> **5–9:** powerful verbs linked to character
> **10:** checking punctuation

8   X DEFINITIVE ANSWER   X SAMPLE ANSWER

A   WARM-UP

Complete the sentence.

1 As _Leah began to sing,_

people stopped what they were doing.

2 If _Luke did not turn the tap off,_

there would be water everywhere.

3 Before _Molly could say anything,_

the old man had gone.

Two words in the list have more than one meaning.
Underline them.

4 stairs <u>table</u> today <u>form</u> sheep

5 <u>pop</u> grape basket east <u>train</u>

6 door <u>letter</u> flour <u>safe</u> large

Add the missing letters.   *Clue: traditional tales*

7 f a b l e

8 m <u>y</u> t h

9 l e <u>g</u> e n d

10 p a r <u>a</u> b l e

> **PART A Focus**
> **1–3:** varying sentence construction; using commas
> **4–6:** homonyms
> **7–10:** topic words (stories); spelling strategies

B   WORD WORK

Write two more words starting with the same prefix.

1 **misunderstand** _misfortune_   _misbehave_

2 **replay** _rebound_   _repay_

3 **internet** _international_   _interview_

What do the prefixes mean?

4 **mis** means _wrong_

5 **re** means _again_

6 **inter** means _between_

> **PART B Focus**
> **1–6:** meaning of prefixes
> **7–8:** rules for adding y
> **9–10:** synonyms; powerful verbs

7 Add the suffix **y.**

ice _icy_   **spike** _spiky_

shine _shiny_   **grease** _greasy_

8 What spelling rule did you use?

Drop the final 'e' to add 'y'.

Write three words you could use to show that someone was

9 speaking **happily.**

smiled   _giggled_   _joked_

10 speaking **fearfully.**

shrieked   _screamed_   _screeched_

C   SENTENCE WORK

Write the sentence in the future tense.

1 **Today the team trains hard.** Tomorrow the _team will train hard._

2 **Today they are friends.** Tomorrow _they will be friends._

3 **Today it is sunny.** Tomorrow _it will be sunny._

Underline the adverb.

4 A light shone <u>faintly</u> in the distance.

5 He played the violin <u>badly</u>.

6 "Come here," he said <u>crossly</u>.

7 Why do we use adverbs?   _They give extra information that is vital to describing the action._

> **PART C Focus**
> **1–3:** future tense
> **4–7:** identifying adverbs and their purpose
> **8–10:** speech marks, capital letters, commas

Add the missing punctuation and capital letters to these newspaper quotes.

8 ᴹmr ᴮbrown told our reporter, "I don't know what all the fuss is about."

9 ᴹmiss ˢshah said, "I think it is a real pity. ᵂwhat are we supposed to do?"

10 ˢsergeant ᴹmoore said, "ᵂwe are looking into what happened."

A   WARM-UP

Write four sentences using some of these words only.

he they sell sells bake bakes bread

1 He sells bread.

2 He bakes bread.

3 They sell bread.

4 They bake bread.

Use these prefixes and suffixes and the word **forget** to make four new words.

un ful able ly

5 forgetful

6 unforgettable

7 forgettable

8 forgetfully

> **PART A Focus**
> 1–4: grammatical agreement
> 5–8: word structure; spelling rules for adding suffixes
> 9–10: spelling strategies; syllables

Write in the missing syllables.

9 con ver sa tion   *Clue: chat, talk*

10 in ves ti ga tion   *Clue: study, enquiry*

B   WORD WORK

Add the suffix that makes the words into adverbs.

1 neat ly   soft ly   sad ly

2 weary ily   happy ily

3 gentle y   idle y

4 Write the root word.

creation   create   **ability**   able

apologise   apology   **flatten**   flat

Use one of the eight words above to complete the sentence.

5 They will flatten the factory and build houses.

6 I must apologise for the noise.

7 It will create chaos in the town centre.

8 He is a very able pupil.

> **PART B Focus**
> 1–3: spelling rules for adding ly
> 4–8: word structure and meaning
> 9–10: distinguishing homophones

Write in the missing word.

sea see hole whole

9 I went to see the blue, blue sea .

10 The whole town gathered round the big hole .

C   SENTENCE WORK

Use one of these connecting words to join the two parts of the sentence.

> **PART C Focus**
> 1–4: connectives; extending sentences
> 5–7: powerful verbs
> 8–10: commas

who when whenever whether

1 It was late when we arrived home.

2 They were going out whether it rained or not.

3 It was Mr Levi who found the missing picture.

4 People can use the gym whenever they want.

Rewrite the sentence using a more powerful verb.

5 He asked for the money.   He demanded the money.

6 He put the ball into the back of the net.   He struck the ball into the back of the net.

7 He made his way through the crowd.   He forced his way through the crowd.

Add commas.

8 At the station he bought a ticket, checked the time of the train and waited on the platform.

9 He ducked under the barrier, dodged behind the fence, scrambled over it and emerged here.

10 Why are the commas needed? To separate the different actions.

X DEFINITIVE ANSWER   X SAMPLE ANSWER

Section 1 Test 8

A WARM-UP

Continue the sentence using a powerful verb.

1 The thunder _rumbled in the distance._

2 The flames _crept closer._

3 Shadows _danced on the walls._

Add the suffix **y** and write the new word.

4 **guilt** _guilty_

5 **sparkle** _sparkly_

6 **nut** _nutty_

PART A Focus
1–3: powerful verbs
4–6: spelling rules for adding y
7: word classes
8–10: fact and opinion

7 What sort of words have you made?
Underline the correct answer.

nouns   **verbs**   **adjectives**

Is the statement a fact or an opinion?

8 Matthews was the best player
on the pitch.   _opinion_

9 Paris is the capital city of France.   _fact_

10 Everyone loves the snow.   _opinion_

B WORD WORK

Underline the word in **bold** that fits the sentence.

1 It was a **super supper** day out.

2 It tasted **biter bitter**.

3 We had **diner dinner** at six.

4 How did you know how each word sounds?
A short vowel is followed by two
consonants and a long vowel by one.

5 Add the correct suffix to make the words
into adjectives.

al ic y ing

rhythm _ic_   sensation _al_

music _al_   sport _y_

athlete _ic_   amaze _ing_

PART B Focus
1–4: double and single consonants
5–8: word structure and meaning
9–10: synonyms for common verbs

Write the words as pairs of near synonyms.

6 _rhythmic_   and _musical_

7 _sporty_   and _athletic_

8 _sensational_ and _amazing_

Write three synonyms.

9 **run** _sprint_   _jog_   _scamper_

10 **walk** _stroll_   _saunter_   _stride_

C SENTENCE WORK

Choose an adverb to add to the sentence.

gracefully neatly excitedly tearfully

1 The crowd shouted _excitedly_ .

2 He folded the clothes _neatly_ .

3 The Princess begged _tearfully_ .

4 The dancer curtseyed _gracefully_ .

5 Put the phrases in order, using 1 for the shortest amount of time and 4 for the longest.

an hour passed   _3_   **a few days later**   _4_

after a few seconds _1_   **minutes ticked by** _2_

PART C Focus
1–4: choosing adverbs
5–6: time, connecting phrases
7–10: future tense

6 Write two phrases showing that even more time has passed.
several weeks afterwards   _nearly a year passed by_

Complete these predictions about your future.

7 Tomorrow I _will get up early._

8 Later this week I _will go to the cinema._

9 Later today I _will watch TV._

10 Next week I _will work harder._

X DEFINITIVE ANSWER   X SAMPLE ANSWER

11

Section 1 Test 9

A WARM-UP

Complete the sentence using alliteration like this.

Rabbits run rapidly over rocks.

1 Snakes *slither speedily over soil.*
2 Cats *creep craftily into corners.*
3 Bears *bounce boldly on beds.*
4 Goats *gobble greedily all the grass.*

These compound words are mixed up.
Write them correctly.

takeboard skatewood

everaway firelasting

5 *takeaway*
6 *everlasting*
7 *skateboard*
8 *firewood*

> **PART A Focus**
> **1–4:** alliteration; using adverbs
> **5–8:** compound words
> **9–10:** synonyms

Write three synonyms.

9 **shout** *yell* *cry* *call*
10 **ate** *gobbled* *munched* *scoffed*

B WORD WORK

Write the past tense.

1 **signal** *signalled*
2 **marry** *married*
3 **buy** *bought*
4 **find** *found*

> **PART B Focus**
> **1–4:** regular and irregular past tense verbs
> **5–7:** suffixes
> **8–10:** meaning of adverbs

Underline the word that is **not** a real word.

5 membership <u>homeship</u> championship
6 movement statement <u>notement</u> argument
7 fitness <u>hateness</u> calmness smoothness

Write a definition of the adverb.

8 Books were scattered **haphazardly**.

haphazardly: *all over the place*

9 Far away an owl hooted **mournfully**.

mournfully: *sadly*

10 He waved his arms **frantically**.

frantically: *madly, anxiously*

C SENTENCE WORK

Write in each space a verb or an adjective that makes the character sound **pleasant**.

1 Mr Hawkins *smiled* at me with his *twinkling* eyes.
2 His voice was *soft* and his manner *calming* .

> **PART C Focus**
> **1–4:** selecting words for effect
> **5–7:** complex sentences
> **8–10:** writing and punctuating dialogue

Write in each space a verb or an adjective that makes the character sound **unpleasant**.

3 Mr Hawkins *glared* at me with his *piercing* eyes.
4 His voice was *harsh* and his manner *blunt* .

Continue the sentence.

5 Before you open the door, *check that there is no-one behind it.*
6 If you are ill, *take things easy for a few days.*
7 Since the adventure playground opened, *it has proved to be very popular.*

Rewrite as dialogue these lines from a play.

8 **Mrs Jones:** I know I had a ticket. *"I know I had a ticket," said Mrs Jones.*
9 **Lee** (*helpfully*): Perhaps it's in your pocket. *"Perhaps it's in your pocket," said Lee, helpfully.*
10 **Mrs Jones** (*thinking*): My pocket … No, it's not in my pocket.

"My pocket," thought Mrs Jones. "No, it's not in my pocket."

X DEFINITIVE ANSWER X SAMPLE ANSWER

Section 1   Test 10

A   WARM-UP

Complete the sentence.

1 The old man looked up at the _____

moon *in the dark sky.*

2 In the morning, the _____ snow

began to fall more quickly.

3 The children jumped over the _____ waves

as they splashed onto the beach.

Write two synonyms.

4 **sadly**   *miserably*   *unhappily*

5 **happily**   *cheerfully*   *joyfully*

6 **quickly**   *rapidly*   *swiftly*

Sort these verbs into pairs showing present and past tenses of the same verb.

get go wear wind

wore got wound went

7 *get*   *got*

8 *go*   *went*

9 *wear*   *wore*

10 *wind*   *wound*

> **PART A Focus**
> **1–3:** sentence formation
> **4–6:** synonyms for adverbs; suffixes
> **7–10:** irregular verbs; past tense

B   WORD WORK

What features do all the words share?

sudden pillow better happy common

1 *a double consonant in the middle*

2 *a short vowel sound before the*
double letters

3 *two syllables*

Underline the prefix and/or suffix. Then write the root word.

4 <u>un</u>natural   *nature*

5 foolish<u>ness</u>   *fool*

6 <u>dis</u>appear<u>ance</u>   *appear*

> **PART B Focus**
> **1–3:** words with double consonants
> **4–6:** word structure; root words
> **7–10:** meaning of homophones

Write a definition of the word in **bold**.

7 **piece**: *a part or bit of something*

peace: *calm quietness*

8 **great**: *wonderful*

grate: *shred into bits (or part of a fire)*

9 **new**: *the latest*

knew: *was familiar with*

10 What do you notice about the pairs of words?
They sound the same but have different
meanings and spellings.

C   SENTENCE WORK

Add a phrase between the commas to say **who** the person is.

1 Mrs Manku, _____*our headteacher*_____ , is a very kind person.

2 Ivan, _____*the farmer's son*_____ , sat in the sunshine.

3 Megan Matthews, _____*my next-door neighbour*_____ , enjoys dancing and singing.

4 Mr Neil, _____*a retired police officer*_____ , was taken to Morton Hospital.

Trim the sentence to the smallest possible number of words. Cross out the extra words.

5 ~~And then just at that moment a loud~~ ^A^ dog barked. ~~noisily somewhere.~~

6 ~~So~~ Oliver ~~just~~ ran. ~~away as fast as he could.~~

7 ~~It seemed like~~ ^M^ many hours passed. ~~with nothing happening.~~

Continue the sentence so that it sounds like a recipe.

8 Gradually *beat in the eggs.*

9 Carefully *stir the sugar.*

10 Slowly *add the milk.*

> **PART C Focus**
> **1–4:** using commas to insert additional information
> **5–7:** effective editing of sentences
> **8–10:** using imperatives in instructions

Section 1 Test 11

A WARM-UP

Write a pair of lines that end with the rhyming words given.

1 Once there was a little green _____ frog

Who always sat on his favourite _____ log.

2 Eve's old rusty _____ car

Takes her near and takes her _____ far.

Add the second syllable.

3 stag _ger_   **Clue:** to sway or lurch

4 tor _rent_   **Clue:** gush of water

5 ten _nis_   **Clue:** a sport

Use the letters to make five past-tense words.

br c f t th aught ought

6 brought

7 caught

8 fought

9 taught

10 thought

> **PART A Focus**
> **1–2:** rhyming couplets
> **3–5:** spelling strategy; word meanings
> **6–10:** irregular verbs; past tense

B WORD WORK

1 Add the same suffix to all the words.

govern _ment_   encourage _ment_

announce _ment_   enjoy _ment_

Use the words in these sentences.

2 The ___government___ made an ___announcement___ .

3 He needed ___encouragement___ to begin with.

4 They got great ___enjoyment___ from the show.

5 Write two more words with the same suffix.

employment   _statement_

> **PART B Focus**
> **1–5:** suffixes; word meanings
> **6–10:** common letter patterns

Write three words with the letter string.

6 ough	cough	rough	tough
7 kn	know	knot	knee
8 ble	table	cable	noble
9 ound	found	round	sound
10 igh	high	night	bright

C SENTENCE WORK

Rewrite each pair of sentences as one sentence. Use an adverb in place of the second sentence.

1 He stamped his foot. He was angry.   He stamped his foot angrily.

2 He turned away. He was sad.   He turned away sadly.

3 He faced the tiger. He was brave.   Bravely, he faced the tiger.

4 No-one saw him. He was lucky.   Luckily, no-one saw him.

> **PART C Focus**
> **1–4:** using adverbs in sentences
> **5–8:** past and future tense
> **9–10:** proper nouns; capital letters

Complete the sentence.

Today I feel happy.

5 Yesterday I ___felt___ happy.

6 Tomorrow I ___will feel___ happy.

Today it is raining.

7 Yesterday it ___was___ raining.

8 Tomorrow it ___will be___ raining.

Cross out the nouns and replace them with proper names.

9 ~~The girl~~ hurried down ~~the street~~ to meet ~~her friend.~~   Ella   Park Street   Marie

10 ~~The man,~~ who lives in ~~the town,~~ had just popped into ~~the shop~~ to buy ~~a newspaper.~~

Mr Snell   Bury   Star News   The Daily Record

☒ DEFINITIVE ANSWER   ☒ SAMPLE ANSWER

Section 1   Test 12

A   WARM-UP

Add details about two different settings.

1 He passed the _cow shed_ where the _farmer_ was _milking the cows._

2 He passed the _garage_ where the _mechanic_ was _trying to fix a broken down van._

Underline the odd one out.

> **PART A Focus**
> **1–2:** precise nouns; setting
> **3–5:** homophones
> **6–8:** punctuating speech
> **9–10:** fact and opinion

3 you ewe <u>your</u> yew

4 too two to <u>tow</u>

5 What makes these the odd ones out?
All the other words are homophones.

Complete the sentence.

6 _"What time is it?"_ asked Mikey.

7 _"Help!"_ screamed Shelley.

8 _"Can you see anything?"_ whispered Doug.

Is the statement a fact or an opinion?

9 The Moon orbits the Earth.   _fact_

10 The Moon is a fascinating place.   _opinion_

B   WORD WORK

Underline the correct spelling.

1 swalow swolow swollow <u>swallow</u>

2 <u>rotten</u> rottun roten rottern

3 kettel ketle <u>kettle</u> kettul

Change the word into a verb by adding a suffix.

> **PART B Focus**
> **1–3:** spelling patterns
> **4–9:** suffixes; word meanings
> **10:** onomatopoeia

4 **pure**   _purify_

5 **modern**   _modernise_

6 **straight**   _straighten_

Use each verb in one of the sentences.

7 There are plans to _modernise_ the station.

8 Filtering helps to _purify_ the water.

9 Stand up and _straighten_ your legs.

10 Write four onomatopoeic words.
hiss   _screech_   _crunch_   _plop_

C   SENTENCE WORK

Cross out some words so that the sentence sounds like a headline.

> **PART C Focus**
> **1–3:** editing; writing headlines
> **4–6:** checking punctuation
> **7–10:** imperative verbs in instructions; precise verb choice

1 ~~Last night~~ City ~~managed to~~ win ~~a match~~ at last.

2 ~~Local people joined together to~~ protest over ~~a possible~~ school closure.

3 ~~An elderly lady called~~ Lily strikes it lucky ~~by winning the lottery.~~

Rewrite the sentence with the correct punctuation marks and capital letters.

4 **Sadly Mr Cohen, shook his head. And turned away**
Sadly, Mr Cohen shook his head and turned away.

5 **"Im' cold. said Ellie,"**   _"I'm cold," said Ellie._

6 **"Neil Adams. aged ten. saw what happened, I phoned the police, at once he said,"**
Neil Adams, aged ten, saw what happened. "I phoned the police at once," he said.

Add a verb to complete these instructions for taking a penalty.

7 _Place_ the ball on the penalty spot.

8 _Look_ at the target.

9 _Strike_ the ball cleanly.

10 _Aim_ for the top corner.

Schofield & Sims English Skills 3

Section 1 Writing task assessment sheet: Saved by a superhero!

Name		Class/Set
Teacher's name		Date

Sentence structure and punctuation

	Always/often	Sometimes	Never
Uses some compound and extended sentences			
Chooses varied conjunctions (e.g., **while**, **but**)			
Varies sentence openings, not always starting with subject			
Demarcates sentences accurately			
Uses capital letters for names, places, dates			
Uses commas to mark grammatical boundaries (e.g., to separate phrases or embedded clauses)			
Chooses appropriate tense (mainly past, also present and future)			
Uses speech marks for quotes			

Composition and effect

Newspaper format maintained (e.g., headlines, quotes)			
Content appropriately organised (e.g., lead sentence or overview, paragraphs describing main events)			
Events developed through a series of linked sentences			
Connectives signal when and/or where			
Some evidence of 'reporter's voice' (e.g., use of adverbs to comment)			
Precise word choice (e.g., proper nouns)			
Appropriate adjectives and verbs chosen for effect			

Spelling

Phonically regular words spelt correctly			
Two- and three-syllable words correct			
Two-syllable words with double consonants correct			
High- and medium-frequency words spelt correctly, including tricky words			
Words with prefixes and/or suffixes correct			
Verb endings **ing** and **ed** correct			
Irregular verbs correct			
Spelling of plurals correct			
Apostrophe used in contracted forms			

Writing task summary

From: **English Skills 3 Answers** by Carol Matchett (ISBN 978 07217 1183 6). Copyright © Schofield & Sims Ltd, 2011. Published by Schofield & Sims Ltd, Dogley Mill, Fenay Bridge, Huddersfield HD8 0NQ, UK (www.schofieldandsims.co.uk). **This page may be photocopied for use within your school or institution only.**

Schofield & Sims English Skills 3

Section 1 Completed proofreading task: The man with the tall hat

Name		Class/Set
Teacher's name		Date

Harry hurrid through the crowdid london streets. he was folowing the man

with the tall hat and woodern cane. he new he must be carefull or he

woud lose him in the crowd.

Harry had cold feet becawse he didnt have eny shoos on. and the grownd

was icey. He trod in some rottun fruit. that had fell of a barow. A carriage

drived by and splash him.

Sudenley, as they went rownd a corna, the man stoped and turnd to

fase harry. "I think you're folowing me, lad. What are you up to?" the man

asked Harry gruffley.

Harry trembeled, wile the man peered at him. with pityless iyes.

Proofreading task summary

Section 1 tasks summary

From: **English Skills 3 Answers** by Carol Matchett (ISBN 978 07217 1183 6). Copyright © Schofield & Sims Ltd, 2011. Published by Schofield & Sims Ltd, Dogley Mill, Fenay Bridge, Huddersfield HD8 0NQ, UK (www.schofieldandsims.co.uk). **This page may be photocopied for use within your school or institution only.**

Section 2 Test 1

A WARM-UP

Complete the sentences.

1 The old man _grumbled about the news._

2 _The hippo_ wallowed _in the mud._

Write in extra letters to make a word.

3 h _a_ p p y

4 _s_ i l l y

5 l i t t _l_ e

6 m _e_ s s _y_

> **PART A Focus**
> 1–2: sentence construction
> 3–7: double consonant spellings
> 8–10: alliteration; adverbs

7 Cross out the words that are wrong.
Write them correctly.

The ~~super~~ tasted ~~biter.~~ _supper_ _bitter_

Continue the sentence like this.

Gary and Grace gobble greedily.

8 Harry and _Holly hop happily._

9 Robbie and _Rachel row rapidly._

10 Salma and _Stella swim steadily._

B WORD WORK

1 Add one suffix and write the new word.

al ary ic

post _postal_   **history** _historic_

diction _dictionary_

Use each word in one of these sentences.

2 It was an _historic_ victory.

3 I looked it up in the _dictionary_ .

4 It was a _postal_ competition.

Write the past tense.

5 **think**   _thought_

6 **fight**   _fought_

7 **buy**   _bought_

> **PART B Focus**
> 1–4: adding suffixes;
> word meanings
> 5–7: irregular past tense
> verbs
> 8–10: meaning of verbs;
> writing definitions

Write a definition.

8 **memorise:** _learn something by heart_

9 **persuade:** _convince someone so that they_
agree with you

10 **supervise:** _watch over_

C SENTENCE WORK

Write a sentence using the adverb.

1 **cheerfully**   _The boy called cheerfully to his friend._

2 **nervously**   _Nervously, they waited for the show to begin._

3 **menacingly**   _The lion stared menacingly._

4 Why do we use adverbs like these?   _They help describe people's feelings._

5 Add the missing commas.

Mrs Lucas, the headteacher, was not very pleased.

6 How did you know where to put the commas?

The commas separate the extra information added to the sentence.

Write another two sentences that use commas in the same way.

7 _Charlie Jackson, my next-door neighbour, is really funny._

8 _Mr Patel, the baker, won first prize._

Complete the sentence.

> **PART C Focus**
> 1–4: using adverbs, purpose
> and position in sentences
> 5–8: commas to separate
> phrases
> 9–10: extending sentences

9 A bus is a large vehicle _that_ carries passengers.

10 A surgeon is a doctor _who_ does operations.

X DEFINITIVE ANSWER **X SAMPLE ANSWER**

Section 2   Test 2

A   WARM-UP

Underline the correct use of the apostrophe.

1 <u>he's</u>   hop's   hed'   have'nt

2 shell'   <u>she's</u>   shed'   sha'nt

3 <u>hadn't</u>   have'nt   hate's   he ll'

4 What does the apostrophe replace in a shortened form?

Missing letters.

These words and suffixes are mixed up.
Write them correctly.

premierment stateness calmable forgetship

5 *premiership*

6 *calmness*

7 *statement*

8 *forgettable*

Cross out the nouns. Write new nouns that make the sentence different.

9 ~~Smoke~~ was drifting in the ~~breeze~~.

Seaweed   *surf*

10 The ~~alien~~ had green ~~scales~~.

singer   *hair*

> **PART A Focus**
> 1–4: apostrophes in short forms
> 5–8: suffixes
> 9–10: precise choice of nouns

B   WORD WORK

Write two words that are linked to the words shown.

1 **medicine**   *medic*   *medical*

2 **memory**   *memorise*   *remember*

3 **horror**   *horrific*   *horrify*

4 Write the correct ending to complete the word.

tch dge

b r i *dge*   p a *tch*

w e *dge*   n u *dge*

h i *tch*   n o *tch*

> **PART B Focus**
> 1–3: root words
> 4–6: common spelling patterns
> 7–10: meaning of adverbs; synonyms

Write three more words with each ending.

5 **tch**   *catch*   *watch*   *itch*

6 **dge**   *edge*   *hedge*   *badge*

Match the adverb to its nearest synonym.

firmly gloomily pleasantly precisely

7 miserably   *gloomily*

8 securely   *firmly*

9 exactly   *precisely*

10 agreeably   *pleasantly*

C   SENTENCE WORK

Add the punctuation to this playscript.

> **PART C Focus**
> 1–3: punctuation, including commas and brackets
> 4–7: adjectives for effect
> 8–10: expanding notes into sentences

1 **Merlin** (*looking up*): Is that you, boy?

2 **Boy** (*nervously*): Yes, sir. It is I.

3 **Merlin:** Good. Well, come here.

4 Underline the adjectives that tell you about the setting.

The surface of the planet was an <u>icy</u> desert, <u>bare</u> and <u>featureless</u>.

5 How do the words make you feel about the planet?

They make it sound an unwelcoming place.

6 Underline the adjectives in this sentence.

The surface of the planet was covered with <u>glistening</u> snow, <u>soft</u>, <u>smooth</u> and <u>untouched</u>.

7 How is this version different?   *The planet sounds beautiful and welcoming.*

Write each note as a complete sentence.

8 **spiders webs food**   *Spiders build webs to catch food.*

9 **stomach – food digested**   *Food is digested in the stomach.*

10 **emu – large bird, run not fly**   *The emu is a large bird that can run, but it cannot fly.*

X DEFINITIVE ANSWER   X SAMPLE ANSWER

19

Section 2   Test 3

A   WARM-UP

Write the notes as two complete sentences.

leopard – cat family – Asia, forests – climb trees

1 The leopard is a member of the cat family found in Asia.

2 It lives in forests and climbs trees.

3 Cross out one letter to change the tense.

feed meet bite slide

PART A Focus
1–2: fill out notes into complete sentences
3–5: irregular past tense verbs
6–7: single and double consonants
8–10: topic words (plays); spelling

4 Make four past tense verbs.

l k w s ept

Kept   wept   swept   slept

5 Add one letter to complete each past tense verb.

a i

r a n   a te   g a ve   d i d

Add single **p** or double **p**.

6 a pp l e   **7** s t a p l e

Add the missing letters. *Clue: found in a playscript*

8 n a r r a t o r   **10** s c e n e

9 s p e e c h

B   WORD WORK

Add the correct prefix or suffix to the word **honest**. Write the word.

1 Thank you for your honesty .

2 Taking the money was dishonest .

3 Honestly , I forgot all about it.

PART B Focus
1–3: word structure and meaning
4–7: rules for adding vowel suffixes
8–10: word meanings; writing definitions

Complete the word sum.

4 **drive + en =** driven

5 **ignore + ing =** ignoring

6 **arrive + al =** arrival

7 What spelling rule did you use?

Drop the final 'e' when adding a suffix that begins with a vowel.

Write a definition of the adjective.

8 **mobile:** able to move around

9 **innocent:** not guilty of anything

10 **outstanding:** especially good

C   SENTENCE WORK

Add two adverbs that give different effects.

PART C Focus
1–4: adverbs for different effects
5–7: using a comma or full stop
8–10: clauses to explain

1 The audience waited patiently . The audience waited excitedly .

2 He walked slowly down the road. He walked briskly down the road.

3 A light shone brightly . A light shone dimly .

4 Suddenly , a figure appeared. Gradually, a figure appeared.

Add a comma, or a full stop and a capital letter. Give a reason for your choice.

5 Because we were late, the coach had already left.

I have used a comma because it separates two parts of a sentence.

6 They ran outside. The street was full of people.

I have used a full stop because there are two separate sentences.

7 The car sped away, racing round the corner.

I have used a comma because the sentence carries on.

Continue the sentence to explain **why**.

8 A glossary can be helpful if you don't know the meaning of a word.

9 Some people wear glasses to help them see better.

10 There is no life on the Moon because there is no water there.

X DEFINITIVE ANSWER   X SAMPLE ANSWER

Section 2 Test 4

A WARM-UP

Continue the sentence in different ways.

1 Jemma spoke to Amy while _she was waiting for the bus._

2 Jemma spoke to Amy, who _had ignored her all day._

3 Jemma spoke to Amy, although _she was still angry._

Write the root word.

4 **humbly**   _humble_

5 **furious**   _fury_

6 **permission**   _permit_

The same three-letter word completes all the words. Write it in.

7 c o l _our_

8 f a v _our_ i t e

9 f l a v _our_

10 c _our_ a g e

PART A Focus
1–3: using conjunctions to continue sentences
4–6: root words
7–10: common spelling patterns

B WORD WORK

Change each noun into a plural.

1 the **thief**   the three _thieves_

2 the **elf**   the three _elves_

3 **beach** and **cliff**   _beaches_ and _cliffs_

4 **knife** and **fork**   _knives_ and _forks_

Add the suffixes to the adjectives.

er est

5 **brave**   _braver_   _bravest_

6 **rich**   _richer_   _richest_

Use the words in these sentences. You will need to add names as well.

7 _Superman_ was brave but _Robin Hood_ was _braver_ and _St George_ was the _bravest_ of all.

8 _My Uncle Luke_ is rich but _the King_ is _richer_ and _Bill Gates_ is the _richest_ of all.

PART B Focus
1–4: plural spelling rules
5–8: comparatives and superlatives
9–10: synonyms for adverbs

Write two synonyms.

9 **fortunately**   _luckily_   _happily_

10 **unfortunately** _unluckily_ _regretfully_

C SENTENCE WORK

Underline the commas and explain why they are needed.

1 The wind blew, tossing the leaves on the trees. _It separates the parts of the sentence._

2 The boy sat up, rubbed his eyes, stretched and looked around. _They separate the different actions._

PART C Focus
1–4: commas to separate parts of a sentence
5–8: contrasting adjectives
9–10: editing for clarity

3 Mrs Jackson, who lives next door, had a real surprise. _They separate the extra information added to the sentence._

4 Finally, it was time to leave. _It separates the connective from the rest of the sentence._

Suggest two different adjectives to describe

5 **texture**   _rough_   _smooth_

6 **heat**   _warm_   _scorching_

7 **taste**   _bitter_   _sweet_

8 **shape**   _spiky_   _spherical_

Cross out any words that are not needed.

9 ~~The reason why~~ he was angry ~~was~~ because someone had lied.

10 Marble is a ~~sort of very~~ hard ~~type of~~ stone with ~~all sorts of~~ coloured patterns ~~in it~~.

X DEFINITIVE ANSWER   X SAMPLE ANSWER

21

Section 2 Test 5

A WARM-UP

On Friday evening, fire swept through a disused warehouse, threatening nearby homes.

1 This text is from a newspaper report.

2 The verbs used are swept and threatening.

3 The verbs have been chosen because they make the fire sound dangerous.

Carefully, tuck the flap into the slot.

4 This text is from instructions.

5 The adverb used is Carefully.

6 The adverb has been chosen because it tells the reader that this could be tricky.

> PART A Focus
> 1–6: language features of text types
> 7–10: root words and suffixes

The words and suffixes are mixed up.
Write them correctly.

deaf**ity** person**ment** stupid**en** enjoy**al**

7 deafen

8 stupidity

9 personal

10 enjoyment

B WORD WORK

1 Underline the odd one out.
rough tough <u>cough</u> enough

2 In what way are all the words the same?
They all have the same spelling pattern.

3 Why is the odd one out different?
The spelling pattern makes an 'off' sound.

Write the word in three parts.

4 **uncomfortable**   un   comfort   able

5 **disagreeable**   dis   agree   able

6 **purposefully**   purpose   ful   ly

Write two synonyms for the word in **bold**.

7 That was **smart** thinking.
clever   intelligent

8 His clothes were **smart**.
neat   stylish

9 He did **pretty** well.
fairly   quite

10 It was a **pretty** cottage.
beautiful   attractive

> PART B Focus
> 1–3: same letters, different sound
> 4–6: word structure
> 7–10: homonyms, distinguishing meaning by context

C SENTENCE WORK

1 How has the writer changed this sentence?
Slowly, ~~T~~the door opened. ~~slowly.~~   He has moved the adverb to the start of the sentence.

2 Why do you think the writer made this change?   To slowly build suspense.

Rewrite these sentences, changing them in a similar way.

3 He gobbled up all the food greedily.   Greedily, he gobbled up all the food.

4 He climbed into bed wearily.   Wearily, he climbed into bed.

5 He stormed down the road angrily.   Angrily, he stormed down the road.

Add another phrase to say **where**. Start the phrase with one of these words.

on by in

6 They sat under a tree on the bank of the river.

7 They came to a small cottage in the shadow of the mountain.

8 There was a tall tower by the lake.

Complete the sentence.

9 "Put down your weapons!" ordered the commander.

10 "Look out!" yelled the captain.

> PART C Focus
> 1–5: starting sentences with an adverb
> 6–8: phrases to clarify meaning
> 9–10: writing and punctuating dialogue

22   X DEFINITIVE ANSWER   X SAMPLE ANSWER

Section 2 Test 6

A WARM-UP

1 Write a sentence using these words.

cat bowl suitcase

The cat found its bowl hidden behind
the suitcase.

2 Write the same sentence with an adverb added.

Luckily, the cat found its bowl hidden
behind the suitcase.

3 Underline the word that is **not** an adverb.

sadly brightly <u>woolly</u> shamelessly

4 How do you know? It is an adjective, used
to describe an object, not an action.

Make the word into an adverb.

5 rare   rarely   **6** lazy   lazily

Add the missing letters.

PART A Focus
1–2: sentence construction
3–6: adverbs
7–9: spelling strategies
10: alphabetical order

7 f r i g h t <u>e</u> n <u>e</u> d

8 f r a n t <u>i</u> c

9 f r a z z <u>l</u> e d

10 Write the words in alphabetical order.

frantic   frazzled   frightened

B WORD WORK

Use the suffix **ness** to change the adjective
into a noun.

1 lovely   loveliness

2 tidy   tidiness

3 What spelling rule did you use?

Change the 'y' to an 'i'.

Use the suffix **ity** to change the adjective
into a noun.

4 mobile   mobility

5 pure   purity

PART B Focus
1–6: rules for
adding suffixes
7–10: homonyms

6 What spelling rule did you use?

Remove the final 'e' to add a vowel suffix.

Write a definition of the word in **bold**.

7 Who will **present** the trophy?

present: give or hand over

8 This is my birthday **present**.

present: a gift

9 Six people were **present** at the meeting.

present: there, attending

Give one way in which the words are different.

10 They have different meanings.

C SENTENCE WORK

A nasty, horrible, disgusting smell came from the cave.

1 What is wrong with this sentence? There are too many adjectives describing the smell.

2 Write the sentence so that it is more effective. A sickening smell came from the cave.

Improve the sentence by crossing out some of the adjectives.

3 A pale, ~~white, light~~ mist drifted in.

4 The porridge was ~~hot, boiling,~~ steaming.

Reorder the words to make two more sentences.

The sun rose slowly over the village.

5 Slowly, the sun rose over the village.

6 The sun rose over the village slowly.

Darkness slipped silently over the city.

7 Silently, darkness slipped over the city.

8 Darkness slipped over the city silently.

Change the sentence so that it uses a comma instead of **and**.

PART C Focus
1–4: choosing adjectives precisely
5–8: moving adverbs; varying
sentences
9–10: using commas to link parts
of sentences

9 Petals fell, ~~and~~ float^{ing}ed on the breeze.

10 The object whizzed through the air, ~~and~~ ^{spinning}~~spun~~ madly.

Section 2 Test 7

A WARM-UP

Complete the sentence.

1 The car stopped when _it came to the crossroads._

2 The car stopped where _no-one could see it._

3 The car stopped while _the lights were on red._

Read the words from a sign and cross out the word that is wrongly spelt. Write the correct spelling.

4 No children ~~aloud~~.   _allowed_

5 No way ~~threw~~.   _through_

6 Welcome on ~~bored~~.   _board_

7 In what way were all the signs wrong?
   They all used the wrong homophone.

Draw a line to join the antonyms.

8 **certain** — excited
9 **outraged** — unsure
10 **subdued** — calm

PART A Focus
1–3: using conjunctions
4–7: homophones
8–10: antonyms

B WORD WORK

Change the nouns and verbs into plurals.

1 Here is my scarf and my glove.
   Here are my scarves and my gloves.

2 The loaf was on the shelf.
   The loaves were on the shelves.

Add a suffix to make the word an adjective.

al ous ic

3 danger   _dangerous_

4 nature   _natural_

5 enthusiast   _enthusiastic_

PART B Focus
1–2: plural spellings
3–8: word construction; meaning
9–10: adjectives; degrees of intensity

Use the words in these sentences.

6 Wild animals can be _dangerous_ .

7 He is an _enthusiastic_ supporter.

8 It looked like _natural_ woodland.

Write two words that mean

9 **extremely cold:** _freezing_ _bitter_

10 **extremely unsafe:** _dangerous_ _hazardous_

C SENTENCE WORK

How does the change alter the character?

1 Aziz ~~smiled~~ at the others. _glowered_ _It makes the character sound angry rather than happy._

2 The man ~~stormed~~ through door. _sneaked_ _'Stormed' suggests that the character is angry._
   'Sneaked' suggests that he doesn't want to be seen.

Make similar changes to these sentences.

3 "Can I help you?" the man ~~asked~~. _demanded_   **5** He ~~put~~ the book on the table. _flung_

4 Sarah ~~bounced~~ into the room.   _stormed_

PART C Focus
1–5: powerful verbs
6–8: turning notes into complete sentences
9–10: capital letters; sentence punctuation

Write the notes as a complete sentence.

6 **paragraph, sentences, one main idea**
   A paragraph has a number of sentences about one main idea.

7 **thesaurus – synonyms**   _A thesaurus contains lists of synonyms._

8 **glossary – definitions**   _A glossary gives definitions of words._

Correct the punctuation and add capital letters.

9 ~~p~~aris is the capital city of ~~f~~rance, ~~i~~t lies on the ~~r~~iver ~~s~~eine.

10 ~~t~~he first modern ~~o~~lympic games took place in ~~a~~thens in 1896. ~~f~~our years later the games were held in ~~p~~aris.

24   X DEFINITIVE ANSWER   X SAMPLE ANSWER

Section 2   Test 8

A   WARM-UP

Write three sentences using these words only.

late she was frequently

1 Frequently, she was late.

2 She was late frequently.

3 She was frequently late.

4 The same three-letter word completes both these words. Write it in.

m e s s _age_   p a s s _age_

Use the five letters to make a word.

PART A Focus
1–3: moving adverbs; sentence variation
4–7: spelling strategies
8–10: synonyms; vocabulary

5 **g h i n t**   night

6 **g h o r u**   rough

7 **g n o u y**   young

Underline the word that is **not** a synonym.

8 curious odd <u>normal</u> strange

9 distant faraway remote <u>nearby</u>

10 stumble <u>stamp</u> stagger lurch

B   WORD WORK

Complete the word sum.

PART B Focus
1–3: rules for adding suffixes
4–6: root words; word structure
7–10: synonyms; working out meaning; technical verbs

1 **terrify + ed =** _terrified_

2 **forgot + en =** _forgotten_

3 **metal + ic =** _metallic_

Write two words that come from the root word.

4 **edit**   editor   edition

5 **person**   personality   personal

6 **connect**   connective   connection

Write a synonym for each of the words in **bold**.

7 Eyelashes **prevent** dust **entering** the eye.

stop   going into

8 The sound is **produced** by air **vibrating** in the pipes.

made   moving

9 Water is **absorbed** by the roots and **transported** to the leaves.

soaked up   moved

10 Some satellites **orbit** the Earth **transmitting** information.

go round   sending out

C   SENTENCE WORK

Extend the sentence so that it says **where**, **why** and **how**.

1 The man sat quietly on the park bench waiting for his wife.

2 She ran hurriedly up and down the street looking for the correct house.

3 Suddenly, the bike skidded onto the pavement to avoid a speeding car.

Underline the phrase that is written correctly.

PART C Focus
1–3: sentence construction; adding phrases to clarify meaning
4–6: apostrophes for possession
7–10: using comparative adjectives

4 Joes hat   <u>Joe's hat</u>   Joes' hat

5 this mans dog   <u>this man's dog</u>   this mans' dog

6 How did you identify the correctly written phrase?

It uses an apostrophe to show that the hat or dog belongs to the person.

Complete the comparative in an interesting way.

7 He was faster than a rocket zooming through space.

8 He was taller than a city skyscraper.

9 It was colder than the North Pole in a blizzard.

10 It was fiercer than a lion hunting for its dinner.

Section 2   Test 9

A   WARM-UP

1 Write a rhyming couplet.

The poor old driver ran and ran

But could not catch his runaway _____ van.

Cross out one letter to change the tense.

2 ~~bite~~   **3** ~~heard~~   **4** ~~shoot~~

Cross out the nouns. Write new nouns that make the sentence different.

5 There was a ~~cave~~ hidden behind the

~~waterfall.~~   door _____   fireplace

6 Further along the ~~corridor~~ there was a ~~door.~~

street _____   factory

PART A Focus
1: rhyming couplets
2–4: irregular verbs; tense changes
5–6: precise nouns
7: plural spelling rules
8–10: compound words

7 Cross out the words that are wrong. Write them correctly.

two ~~loafs~~ of bread   loaves

three ~~potatos~~   potatoes

three little ~~jellys~~   jellies

Make three compound words.

8 cross word   **10** cross over

9 cross roads

B   WORD WORK

Cross out the words that are wrongly spelt. Write the correct spelling.

1 The ~~refferee~~ ~~blue~~ his ~~whisle.~~
referee _____   blew _____   whistle

2 Three ~~peeple~~ ~~dround~~ ~~yesturday.~~
people _____   drowned _____   yesterday

3 The sheep ~~folowed~~ the ~~babby~~ ~~calfs.~~
followed _____   baby _____   calves

Complete the word sum to make an adjective.

4 **fashion** + able = fashionable

5 **protect** + ive = protective

6 **poet** + ic = poetic

7 **fame** + ous = famous

PART B Focus
1–3: checking spellings
4–7: suffixes; word structure
8–10: definitions; vocabulary

Write a definition of the word in **bold**.

8 This snake is highly **venomous**.
venomous: poisonous

9 This animal is close to **extinction**.
extinction: having died out

10 The creature was most **inquisitive**.
inquisitive: curious

C   SENTENCE WORK

Twigs touched his face like gnarled fingers.

1 Why has the writer used this simile?   To create a frightening effect.

Complete these similes to create a similar mood.

2 The sound of thunder was like a growling monster coming ever closer.

3 The sea was like a boiling cauldron.

4 The cold wind was like icy knives slashing the air.

Cross out the words that are wrong. Write them correctly.

5 The elephant ~~use it's~~ trunk to drink.   uses _____   its

6 Moles ~~is~~ almost blind, but they ~~has~~ very good hearing.   are _____   have

7 A crocodile ~~spend~~ most ~~off it's~~ life in the water.   spends _____   of _____   its

Complete the sentence.

8 "Help me!" screamed Marcie.

9 The old man sighed and said, "I'm sorry. I can't help you."

10 The boy looked pleased and said, "Thank you. That is very helpful."

PART C Focus
1–4: similes
5–7: grammatical accuracy
8–10: punctuating dialogue

X DEFINITIVE ANSWER   X SAMPLE ANSWER

Section 2 Test 10

A WARM-UP

Write the notes as a complete sentence.

1 animals – oxygen – stay alive

All animals need oxygen to stay alive.

2 compass – shows North

A compass is a device that shows the direction of North.

Complete the word sum.

3 **dazzle + ing + ly** = _dazzlingly_

4 **pure + ify + ing** = _purifying_

5 **envy + ous + ly** = _enviously_

Add a short word to complete the longer word.

6 a c c i _dent_

7 c o m f o r _table_

8 b r i l l i _ant_

> **PART A Focus**
> **1–2:** writing notes as complete sentences
> **3–5:** word structure; spelling rules
> **6–8:** spelling strategies
> **9–10:** using adverbs

Complete the sentence.

9 Gradually, _the bucket filled with water._

10 Courageously, _the man faced the lion._

B WORD WORK

Correct the spelling of the word in **bold**.

1 The hailstones **ricoshayed** off the roof.
ricocheted

2 The man was **distrought**. _distraught_

3 The King was rather **pompus**. _pompous_

Write the meaning of each word.

4 'ricocheted': _bounced off_

5 'distraught': _upset or distressed_

6 'pompous': _arrogant_

Complete the word chain. **cold colder coldest**

7 angry _angrier_ _angriest_

8 slim _slimmer_ _slimmest_

9 brave _braver_ _bravest_

> **PART B Focus**
> **1–3:** checking spellings; using a dictionary
> **4–6:** word meanings
> **7–9:** adding er and est
> **10:** adjectives; degrees of intensity

10 Sort the words into two groups.

glad thrilled elated
cheerful ecstatic pleased

quite happy: _glad_ _cheerful_ _pleased_

extremely happy: _thrilled_ _elated_ _ecstatic_

C SENTENCE WORK

1 Compare these two sentences. Underline the words that are different.

White, <u>fluffy</u> clouds <u>floated gently</u> above them. <u>Dark, sinister</u> clouds <u>hung heavily</u> above them.

2 How do the changes affect the mood? _The words in the first sentence create a happy mood. The words in the second sentence create a threatening mood._

Cross out the verbs and/or adjectives. Write new words that change the mood.

3 The trees ~~whispered~~ and ~~fluttered~~ their leaves. _moaned_ _shook_

4 A ~~bright, cheery~~ light ~~flooded~~ the windows. _dim_ _murky_ _crept through_

Rewrite the phrase using three words only.

5 the coat belonging to the girl _the girl's coat_

6 the hair belonging to the teacher _the teacher's hair_

7 the cloak belonging to the actor _the actor's cloak_

> **PART C Focus**
> **1–4:** expressive language; creating mood
> **5–7:** possessive apostrophes
> **8–10:** using connectives to link events

Complete the second sentence.

8 The door closed. A moment later, _all the lights went out._

9 First, food is chewed. Next, _it is swallowed._

10 There was a flash of lightning. One second later, _there was a clap of thunder._

Section 2   Test 11

A   WARM-UP

1 Write a rhyming couplet.

Marek, Lucy, Nell and Pete

Live in houses on my _____ street.

Write two synonyms.

2 **sly**   cunning   sneaky

3 **fragile**   delicate   breakable

4 Add adjectives.

He was wearing   tatty   trousers,

a stained T-shirt and scruffy shoes.

5 Add different adjectives to change the picture.

He was wearing baggy trousers,

a colourful T-shirt and   red   shoes.

Add the same prefix to all the words.

6 dis loyal

7 dis like

8 dis infect

9 dis honest

> **PART A Focus**
> **1:** rhyming couplets
> **2–5:** synonyms; adjectives
> **6–9:** prefixes
> **10:** alphabetical order

10 Write the words in alphabetical order.

dishonest disinfect dislike   disloyal

B   WORD WORK

Underline the word that is not often used today.

1 It is said that a strange old lady dwells

in the woods.

2 He held the sword aloft.

Write a definition of each word that you underlined.

3 'dwells'   means   lives

4 'aloft'   means   high

> **PART B Focus**
> **1–4:** archaic words
> **5–7:** spelling of tricky words
> **8–10:** prefixes

Underline the correct spelling.

5 diffrent **different** diffarent differrent

6 speshial spectial special speciall

7 properly propperly properley propurly

Add the same prefix to all three words.

8 ad jective   ad verb   ad mire

9 al most   al ready   al ways

10 a board   a blaze   a part

C   SENTENCE WORK

Write the start and the end of the sentence.

1 For six hours   the plane waited to take off.

2 Just then   Alia walked in with a letter in her hand.

3 All at once   the balloon burst and fell to the ground.

It is a lovely day as Miles starts his walk.

4 This sentence is from a story. Why does it sound wrong for a story?

It is written in the present tense rather than the past tense.

5 Write it correctly.   It was a lovely day as Miles started his walk.

> **PART C Focus**
> **1–3:** sentence construction
> **4–7:** past and present tense
> **8–10:** checking punctuation

Trees lost their leaves in autumn.

6 This sentence is from an information text. Why does it sound wrong?

It is written in the past tense rather than the present tense.

7 Write it correctly.   Trees lose their leaves in autumn.

Proofread and correct the text.

8 "What flavour ice-cream does you want? There is mint or vanilla," explained Jodie.

9 Which is your favourite colour? Is it red, blue, yellow or green?

10 "Stop!" screamed Gus. "Don't do it!"

X DEFINITIVE ANSWER   X SAMPLE ANSWER

Section 2   Test 12

A   WARM-UP

Write three sentences using these words only.

slowly spoke Lila

1	Lila spoke slowly.
2	Lila slowly spoke.
3	Slowly, Lila spoke.

PART A Focus
1–3: sentence variation
4–6: apostrophe in shortened forms
7–10: suffixes

Complete the table.

	you've	you have
4	they'd	they would or they had
5	shan't	shall not
6	we're	we are

Underline the word that you **cannot** add the suffix to.

7 **ic** atom <u>plural</u> angel poet

8 **al** occasion nation addition <u>reaction</u>

9 **ness** fit <u>might</u> pure like

10 **able** avoid bend <u>mess</u> read

B   WORD WORK

Write the past tense.

1 **teach** taught   2 **wind** wound

3 Complete the word sum.

fast + er = faster

PART B Focus
1–2: spelling of irregular past tense verbs
3–8: comparatives and superlatives
9–10: synonyms

4 What happens when you add **er** to an adjective?

It makes it into a comparative.

5 Complete the word sum.

fast + est = fastest

6 What happens when you add **est** to an adjective?

It makes it into a superlative.

7 Underline the adjective that you **cannot** add **er** and **est** to.

hard <u>difficult</u> tough clear

8 Why can you not add **er** or **est**?

They only work with short adjectives.
With longer words you use 'more'
or 'most'.

Write three synonyms.

9 **eerie** spooky   creepy   weird

10 **hazy** misty   foggy   smoky

C   SENTENCE WORK

Write the opening sentence for

PART C Focus
1–3: opening sentences
4–7: similes
8–10: writing and punctuating dialogue

1 **a report on the five senses.**

We all have five senses to help us find out about the world around us.

2 **a local newspaper report on a school fete.**

Last Saturday, Park Lane Primary School held a very successful Summer Fete.

3 **an explanation of how a torch works.** A torch is a handheld device for giving light.

Complete the simile.

4 Mrs Warrington's hat looked like a wedding cake.

5 The snow on the ground looked like a white duvet spread over the world.

6 The roof of the building was shaped like an onion.

7 The alien's teeth were like daggers.

Write the sentence as a line of dialogue.

8 Ben asked Alia for help.   "Alia, can you help me?" asked Ben.

9 Josh shouted hello to Ravi.   "Hello, Ravi!" shouted Josh.

10 I asked the man his name.   "What is your name?" I asked the man.

Remind the pupil to complete Section 2 of the Progress chart on page 46 of the workbook.   29

Schofield & Sims English Skills 3

Section 2 Writing task assessment sheet: Jen's computer adventure

Name			Class/Set	
Teacher's name			Date	

Sentence structure and punctuation

	Always/often	Sometimes	Never
Uses varied sentence structure			
Extends sentences to give detail (e.g., by using adverbs)			
Uses various subordinating connectives (e.g., **although**, **until**, **where**)			
Varies sentence openings (e.g., by starting with a conjunction or adverb)			
Demarcates sentences accurately			
Uses speech marks for direct speech			
Uses commas to mark phrases and clauses			
Uses correctly the possessive apostrophe			

Composition and effect

Setting presented to interest reader			
Story shaped round events (e.g., new paragraph for new event or different focus)			
Atmosphere described using expressive language			
Connecting or adverbial phrases link ideas and events			
Vocabulary (including similes) chosen for effect			
Expanded noun phrases and adjectives add detail			
Powerful verbs chosen for impact			

Spelling

Phonically regular words spelt correctly			
Words with double consonants spelt correctly			
Common letter strings spelt correctly (e.g., **ough**, **tch**)			
Tricky high- and medium-frequency words correct			
Applies rules for adding prefixes and suffixes			
Applies rules for adding verb endings			
Irregular verbs correct			
Applies rules for spelling plurals			
Apostrophe used in contracted forms			
Common homophones correct			

Writing task summary

From: **English Skills 3 Answers** by Carol Matchett (ISBN 978 07217 1183 6). Copyright © Schofield & Sims Ltd, 2011. Published by Schofield & Sims Ltd, Dogley Mill, Fenay Bridge, Huddersfield HD8 0NQ, UK (www.schofieldandsims.co.uk). **This page may be photocopied for use within your school or institution only.**

Schofield & Sims English Skills 3

Section 2 Completed proofreading task: All about spiders

Name		Class/Set
Teacher's name		Date

Spiders are small animuls that have ~~ate~~ [eight] legs. and bodys made up of ~~too~~ [two] rownd secshuns. [a above animuls; ie above bodys; u above rownd; tio above secshuns]

Spiders produce thin threds, wich they use to spin webs. Furst, the spider atachis [a above threds; h above wich; i above Furst; t above atach; e above atachis]

the thred to an object. And then it bilds the web. the web looks like silk. but is [a above thred; a above And; u above bilds; T above the web] much stronger. [e above stronger]

The web is for caching the spiders food. an insect flys into it, get's stuck and struguls [t above caching; A above an; ie above flys; gle above struguls]

to get away. the spider feels the movemunt and rushis out, traping the insect. [T above the; e above movemunt; e above rushis; p above traping]

Spiders live in lots of placis, even peoples housis. The trap door spider hides in a [e above placis; e above housis]

burow waitting for a likly victim. it then pops out and atacks. [r above burow; e above likly; I above it; t above atacks]

althouw spiders have a poisonus bite, ownly a few are harmfull to peeple. the black [A above althouw; gh above althouw; o above poisonus; o above peeple; T above the]

widow can be very danjerus. [g and o above danjerus]

Proofreading task summary

Section 2 tasks summary

From: **English Skills 3 Answers** by Carol Matchett (ISBN 978 07217 1183 6). Copyright © Schofield & Sims Ltd, 2011. Published by Schofield & Sims Ltd, Dogley Mill, Fenay Bridge, Huddersfield HD8 0NQ, UK (www.schofieldandsims.co.uk). **This page may be photocopied for use within your school or institution only.**

Section 3 Test 1

A WARM-UP

Complete the sentence to explain what happens.

1 When we breathe in, _air enters our lungs._

2 As we grow, _we get taller and stronger._

Add the missing letters.

Clue: one t or two?

> **PART A Focus**
> **1–2:** clauses to explain
> **3–6:** spelling rule; double letters
> **7–10:** suffixes; word structure

3 ro _tt_ en   ti _t_ le

4 wai _t_ er   ki _tt_ en

5 What spelling rule did you use?

If the first vowel is short, use a
double letter.

6 Make some more words that follow this rule.

_ta_ ble   _ru_ bble   _la_ ter   _mu_ tter

Add the same suffix to each word.

7 season _al_   tropic _al_   tradition _al_

8 poet _ic_   class _ic_   organ _ic_

9 wood _en_   gold _en_   moist _en_

10 amaze _ment_   treat _ment_   move _ment_

B WORD WORK

1 Underline the odd one out.

thieves halves <u>beliefs</u> selves

2 It is the odd one out because _most words_
ending with 'f' change to 'ves' when
made plural.

3 Underline the odd one out.

serious curious obvious <u>hideous</u>

4 It is the odd one out because _all the_
others end with 'ious'.

> **PART B Focus**
> **1–4:** spelling rules
> **5–9:** compound words
> **10:** synonyms; word meanings

Make three compound words.

bag base corn data hand pop

5 _handbag_   **7** _popcorn_

6 _database_

Make five compound words starting with

8 **head**   _headline_   _headphones_
       headband   _headlight_   _headroom_

9 **snow**   _snowflake_   _snowman_
       snowboard   _snowball_   _snowdrop_

10 Underline the word that is **not** a synonym.

dependable <u>shameful</u> faithful reliable

C SENTENCE WORK

Add an adverb that says **how** the action is performed.

1 _Slowly,_   they opened the door.

2 _Eagerly,_   they looked in the trunk.

3 _Cautiously,_   they peeped round the corner.

Continue the sentence to say **who** the person is.

4 They took the book to Mr Anderson, _the headteacher._

5 They went to see Old Jack, _who worked on the farm._

6 Our reporter spoke to Agnes Wilson, _the owner of the shop._

7 Why is there a comma ? _To separate the different pieces of information._

Cross out the word that is wrong. Write it correctly.

8 The road is ~~dangerouser~~ now.   _more dangerous_

9 This is the ~~importantest~~ reason.   _most important_

10 This is the ~~goodest~~ idea.   _best_

> **PART C Focus**
> **1–3:** adverbs for clarity
> **4–7:** extending sentences; commas to mark phrases or clauses
> **8–10:** comparatives and superlatives

X DEFINITIVE ANSWER   X SAMPLE ANSWER

Section 3 Test 2

A WARM-UP

Cross out the similes. Write more original similes of your own.

1 As happy as ~~a lark~~ *the owner of a winning lottery ticket.*

2 As brave as ~~a lion~~ *Captain Marvel facing the aliens.*

3 As strong as ~~an ox~~ *six elephants.*

4 Make four compound words.

house horse work power shoe

housework   *workhorse*

horsepower   *horseshoe*

5 Write four compound words using the word **yard**.

boatyard   *churchyard*

courtyard   *farmyard*

> **PART A Focus**
> **1–3:** similes
> **4–5:** compound words
> **6–10:** spelling of homophones

Write the homophone, spelt correctly.

6 **right** *write*   9 **new** *knew*

7 **no** *know*   10 **peace** *piece*

8 **stair** *stare*

B WORD WORK

Complete the table of adjectives.

		comparative	superlative
1	**flat**	flatter	flattest
2	**cheeky**	cheekier	cheekiest
3	**good**	better	best

4 Write the root of the word **pressure**. *press*

5 Write a definition.

pressure: *a force pressing on something*

6 Write another word with the same root.

depress

7 Underline the root word.

<u>block</u>age <u>medicine</u> dis<u>order</u>ly

> **PART B Focus**
> **1–3:** comparatives and superlatives
> **4–7:** root words
> **8–10:** spelling errors

Cross out the words that are wrongly spelt. Write the correct spelling.

8 Rats ~~tunneled~~ into the ~~ansient~~ walls of the ~~casle.~~ *tunnelled   ancient   castle*

9 He had to ~~apolojize~~ to the ~~laddy~~ after the ~~acsident.~~ *apologise   lady   accident*

10 It was ~~impossable~~ to find ~~enythink~~ on the ~~shelfs.~~ *impossible   anything   shelves*

C SENTENCE WORK

Extend the sentence using one of these words to start.

> **PART C Focus**
> **1–3:** extending sentences
> **4–6:** apostrophe for possession
> **7–10:** words chosen for effect

who where that

1 The two friends were so happy *that they could not stop laughing.*

2 She sat next to Aaron and Beth, *who were arguing.*

3 They went to the gates *where they had been told to wait.*

4 **Three boys share a tent.**

Underline the correct phrase.

the boy's tent   <u>the boys' tent</u>

5 **The girl has a tent to herself.**

Underline the correct phrase.

<u>the girl's tent</u>   the girls' tent

6 Give a reason for your answers. *The apostrophe goes after the 's' if the thing belongs to more than one person. It goes before the 's' if it belongs to just one person.*

7 Underline the words that are different.   "Stop," he <u>whispered meekly</u>. "Stop," he <u>said defiantly</u>.

8 In the second sentence the character sounds *braver.*

Change the sentence by using a different word at the end.

9 "I'll take that," she said *spitefully* .

10 "I'll take that," she said *gently* .

Section 3   Test 3

A   WARM-UP

Put the words in order so the sentence makes sense.

1 The ducks fed the children.

The children fed the ducks.

2 The road ran over the squirrel.

The squirrel ran over the road.

3 Many homeless were left survivors.

Many survivors were left homeless.

Write the root word.

4 **argument**   *argue*

5 **discussion**   *discuss*

6 **explanation**   *explain*

> **PART A Focus**
> **1–3:** sentence structure; word order
> **4–7:** root words
> **8–10:** spelling strategies

7 Write two words with the same root as

persuade   *persuasive*   *persuasion*

Add the missing syllables.

8 ex *cla* ma *tion*   **Clue:** *ends with !*

9 al *pha* bet *ic* al   **Clue:** *in letter order*

10 ad *ver* tise *ment*

Clue: *makes you want to buy it*

B   WORD WORK

1 Underline the word that is wrongly spelt.

knight might <u>hight</u> slight

2 Write the correct spelling.   *height*

3 Underline the word that is wrongly spelt.

huff gruff stuff <u>enuff</u>

4 Write the correct spelling.   *enough*

These root words and suffixes are mixed up.
Write them correctly.

photograph**ive** novel**ly** mass**ic** curious**ist**

5 *photographic*

6 *massive*

7 *novelist*

8 *curiously*

> **PART B Focus**
> **1–4:** spelling patterns; exceptions
> **5–8:** suffixes; word structure
> **9–10:** word meanings

Write a definition of the word in **bold**.

9 It was an **indescribable** mess.

indescribable: *beyond words*

10 He spoke **apologetically**.

apologetically: *as if he were sorry*

C   SENTENCE WORK

Why has the writer used an adverb?

1 They whispered anxiously.   *It shows the feelings of the characters.*

2 The wind blew the curtains gently.   *It gives a clearer picture or sense of the wind.*

3 He looked absolutely everywhere.   *It adds emphasis.*

4 Gradually, add the mixture to the pan.   *It says exactly how.*

Add the missing punctuation and capital letters.

5 Although it was dark, we weren't scared. W̌ell, only a bit.

6 "Don't follow me,"Alice shouted, as she strutted off down the street.

7 "Yes, you,"said the voice. Člear off!"

> **PART C Focus**
> **1–4:** adverbs for clarity and emphasis
> **5–7:** checking punctuation
> **8–10:** expressive language to create mood

Rewrite the sentence so it creates an eerie mood.

8 A path twisted through the garden.

An overgrown path twisted through the wild, unwelcoming garden.

9 The castle had stone walls and turrets.

The castle had cold, grey walls and turrets that seemed to stand guard.

10 The river flowed.   *The murky river churned under the darkening clouds.*

X DEFINITIVE ANSWER   X SAMPLE ANSWER

Section 3   Test 4

A   WARM-UP

Write the sentence with the adverb
in a different place.

Nat walked slowly to school.

1 Nat walked to school slowly.

2 Slowly, Nat walked to school.

3 Write a sentence using these words.

scrambled hurriedly

Carly scrambled hurriedly over the rocks.

4 Underline the word that is **not** a comparative.

slower colder <u>runner</u> funnier

5 Explain your answer. 'Runner' does not
describe or compare anything.

6 Make three compound words.

rain water proof fall

rainwater   waterproof   waterfall

Draw a line to join the synonyms.

7 **doubtful** —————— acceptable

8 **shameful** —————— uncertain

9 **heartless** —————— disgraceful

10 **satisfactory** —————— unfeeling

> **PART A Focus**
> **1–3:** using adverbs
> **4–5:** comparative adjectives
> **6:** compound words
> **7–10:** synonyms; word meanings

B   WORD WORK

Add the correct suffix to complete each word.

ible ist able cial tial est

1 par _tial_   spe _cial_   so _cial_

2 horr _ible_   respect _able_   terr _ible_

3 smooth _est_   novel _ist_   dent _ist_

Write a definition.

4 roadworthy: safe to go on the road

5 departure: going away

6 balloonist: someone who flies a hot
air balloon

7 household: the people who live in
a house

> **PART B Focus**
> **1–3:** word endings
> **4–7:** word structure; word meaning
> **8–10:** spelling revision

Cross out the words that are wrongly
spelt. Write the correct spelling.

8 Don't ~~forgget comas~~ when ~~writting~~
~~longger~~ sentences.

forget   commas   writing   longer

9 It ~~mite~~ take ~~for weaks~~ to get ~~their.~~

might   four   weeks   there

10 The three ~~wifes carrid~~ the ~~loafs~~ without
~~droping~~ them.

wives   carried   loaves   dropping

C   SENTENCE WORK

Combine the three sentences into one.

1 He hummed softly. He walked across the field. He went towards the barn.

He hummed softly as he walked across the field towards the barn.

2 Charlie tiptoed down the stairs. His sister heard him. She called out.

Although Charlie tiptoed down the stairs, his sister heard him and called out.

Write a shorter phrase using an apostrophe.

3 the cot belonging to the baby   the baby's cot

4 the coat belonging to that girl   that girl's coat

5 the kit belonging to the team   the team's kit

6 the books belonging to the boys   the boys' books

7 the spaceship belonging to the aliens   the aliens' spaceship

Complete these similes.

8 The wires were twisted   like spaghetti.

9 Blossom fell   like snowflakes.

10 He prowled   like a tiger.

> **PART C Focus**
> **1–2:** composing longer sentences
> **3–7:** apostrophe for possession
> **8–10:** similes

Section 3 Test 5

A WARM-UP

1 Write the diary note as one complete sentence.

woke early – shower, dressed, porridge

I woke early, had a shower, got dressed and had some porridge for breakfast.

Complete the sentence.

2 A squirrel is a small furry animal that
climbs trees.

3 Sammy the squirrel watched while
the other squirrels gathered acorns.

4 Six sad squirrels *slept soundly into spring.*

Underline the word that is **not** a real word.

5 funniest <u>amusingest</u> wittiest silliest

6 speedier <u>difficulter</u> frostier bigger

7 How do you know that the words are
not real? *You should say 'most amusing'
and 'more difficult'.*

PART A Focus
1: writing full sentences from notes
2–4: extending sentences; text types
5–7: comparatives and superlatives
8–10: synonyms

Write two synonyms for the verb.

8 **quake** *shake* *tremble*

9 **confuse** *puzzle* *baffle*

10 **throw** *hurl* *fling*

B WORD WORK

Write in the missing syllables.

1 *sub* trac *tion* **Clue:** *taking away*

2 *sen* sa *tion* al **Clue:** *wonderful, amazing*

3 *su* per *son* ic **Clue:** *faster than sound*

4 Underline the word that is **not** linked by meaning.

triangle tricycle <u>triumph</u> tripod

5 How are the other three words linked?
The 'tri' part of the word means 'three'.

6 Write three words that begin with **micro**.
microscope *microphone* *microwave*

7 What is the meaning of **micro**? *small*

PART B Focus
1–3: spelling strategies; syllables
4–7: common roots; meanings
8–10: its and it's

Write the correct word.

it's its

8 The cat drank *its* milk.

9 Today *it's* going to be sunny.

10 The van has lost *its* wheel and *it's*
going to crash.

C SENTENCE WORK

Write the next three sentences.

Many people would benefit from a new leisure centre.

1 For example, *keep fit classes could be held there.*

2 However, *it would be expensive to build.*

3 Clearly, *it is an important decision.*

Move the commas to the correct places.

4 Mount Everest, the tallest mountain, in the world, is in, the Himalayas.

5 When it reaches boiling point, water, turns to steam.

6 The wind blew, shaking the leaves, on the trees.

Add suitable words.

7 House for sale – this is a *delightful* *detached* house in a *quiet* location.

8 The leaves fell, *floating* and *swirling* to the ground.

9 *Carefully* , fold the card in half.

10 From the *treetop* , he could see the *soldiers* in their *uniforms* .

PART C Focus
1–3: connectives to link ideas
4–6: commas to mark clauses
7–10: word classes; selecting words

X DEFINITIVE ANSWER   X SAMPLE ANSWER

Section 3　Test 6

A　WARM-UP

1　Write a rhyming couplet.

The sun can shine and wind can blow,

These are two of the things I ___ know.

2　What is the root word of **couplet**?

___couple___ , meaning _two of something_

Underline the suffix that you **cannot** add to the word.

3　**correct**　ly　tion　ive　<u>ful</u>

4　**hard**　ly　en　ship　<u>ist</u>　ness

5　**thick**　ly　en　ness　<u>able</u>　est

Add a short word to complete the longer word.

6　f l a v _our_　　**8**　s a v _age_

7　p r a c t _ice_

> **PART A Focus**
> 1–2: rhyming couplets; word play
> 3–5: word structure
> 6–8: spelling strategies
> 9–10: sentence construction

Write a sentence using these words.

9　**murmur　gather**

Outside there was a murmur of voices
as a crowd began to gather.

10　**waited　leaping**

The lion waited patiently before leaping
out onto its prey.

B　WORD WORK

Cross out the word that is wrong.
Write the correct word.

1　Frosty Flakes – a great new ~~serial~~.　_cereal_

2　A choice of colours – red or ~~blew~~.　_blue_

3　Soft as silk for really shiny ~~hare~~.　_hair_

4　Why were the words spelt incorrectly?

Because the wrong homophone was used.

Use two of these suffixes to complete the word sum.

al ic ist ive tion ly

> **PART B Focus**
> 1–4: homophones
> 5–7: adding suffixes
> 8–10: words with multiple meanings

5　**secret**　+ _ive_ + _ly_ = secretively

6　**educate** + _tion_ + _al_ = educational

7　**art**　　+ _ist_ + _ic_ = artistic

Write a synonym for the word in **bold**.

8　a **flat** surface　　_even_

9　a **flat** refusal　　_complete_

10　his voice was **flat**　　_uninteresting_

C　SENTENCE WORK

Change the order of the words to make a question.

1　Anil is going out.　　Is Anil going out?

2　Mr French has seen the garden.　　Has Mr French seen the garden?

3　Leo can go to the cinema.　　Can Leo go to the cinema?

4　Marie went to town on Saturday.　　Did Marie go to town on Saturday?

5　The last question is the odd one out because _you have to add a word ('did')._

Sort the phrases into two groups.

the boy's late, the boy's bag, Mark's room, Mark's sorry, Sophie's gone, Sophie's friend

6　**apostrophes for possession:**　the boy's bag　Mark's room　Sophie's friend

7　**apostrophes for shortened forms:**　the boy's late　Mark's sorry　Sophie's gone

Complete these sentences, which are to describe a new vacuum cleaner.

8　It is speedier than _a Formula One racing car._

9　It is quieter than _a whisper._

10　It is more powerful than _a jet engine._

> **PART C Focus**
> 1–5: turning statements into questions
> 6–7: apostrophes for omission or possession
> 8–10: using comparatives

Section 3 Test 7

A WARM-UP

Continue the sentence to give a clear picture of **where** the event took place.

1 Kelly jumped _over the fence and hid behind the shed._

2 Gareth ran _across the field to the farmhouse._

3 Underline the odd one out.

they can't   he'll help

we're late   <u>Jack's drink</u>

4 Give a reason for your choice.

It uses an apostrophe for possession.

Change the **suffix** to make a new word.

5 **light**ly → _lightness_

6 **worth**y → _worthless_

7 **action** → _active_

> **PART A Focus**
> **1–2:** clarifying events
> **3–4:** using apostrophes
> **5–7:** suffixes
> **8–10:** prefixes; hyphens

Write three words starting with the prefix **non**.

8 _nonsense_   **10** _non-stop_

9 _non-stick_

B WORD WORK

1 Underline the letter string that is found in all these words. <u>hour</u> <u>journey</u> <u>mourn</u>

2 What do you notice about the sounds made?

'our' makes a different sound in each word.

3 Write four more words with this letter string.

flour   _journal_   _pour_   _tourist_

4 Write the suffixes that you can add to the word.

ed ing er est s ly

farm   _ed ing er s_

slow   _ed ing er est s ly_

Add the suffixes to **farm** and **slow** and sort the words into groups.

5 **nouns:**   _farmer_   _farms_

 adverbs: _slowly_

6 **adjectives:** _slower_   _slowest_

7 **verbs:**   _farmed_   _farming_   _farms_

       slowed   _slowing_   _slows_

Draw a line to join the synonyms.

8 **enviously**   clumsily

9 **awkwardly**   firmly

10 **determinedly**   jealously

> **PART B Focus**
> **1–3:** tricky letter strings
> **4–7:** suffixes; word classes
> **8–10:** synonyms; word meanings

C SENTENCE WORK

1 Underline the adjectives.   We are <u>innocent</u> victims of these <u>thoughtless</u> actions.

2 Why have the adjectives been added? _To make the argument stronger._

Add adjectives.

> **PART C Focus**
> **1–4:** adjectives for effect
> **5:** identifying sentence types
> **6–7:** moving phrases; commas
> **8–10:** extending sentences; using commas

3 These _wicked_ people have caused _needless_ suffering.

4 It is a _sad_ fact that many _helpless_ animals are mistreated.

5 Identify the type of sentence. Is it a **question**, **order** or **exclamation**?

What a mess   _exclamation_   Turn that tap off   _order_

Can you help me   _question_

Rewrite the sentence twice, starting with a different word each time.

Raj tried hard but Kaz won.

6 _Although Raj tried hard, Kaz won._   **7** _Kaz won, even though Raj tried hard._

Continue the sentence.

8 Sarah raced after the bus, _waving madly._   **10** Shelley, _who was late, missed the game._

9 We wrote a letter, _asking for permission._

X DEFINITIVE ANSWER   X SAMPLE ANSWER

Section 3 Test 8

A WARM-UP

Continue this rhyme.

PART A Focus
1–4: alliteration; word play
5–7: compound words
8–10: suffixes

Simon sings sweetly on Sundays.

1 Molly _marches madly_ on Mondays.

2 Tarun _talks truthfully_ on Tuesdays.

3 Will _waves wildly_ on Wednesdays.

4 Fred _fishes frantically_ on Fridays.

Write three compound words starting with

5 **down**

downstairs   _downpour_   _downfall_

6 **break**

breakfast   _breakthrough_   _breakwater_

7 **super**

supermarket   _superstar_   _superstore_

Add the same suffix to all three words.

8 friend _ship_   owner _ship_   hard _ship_

9 wash _able_   remark _able_   respect _able_

10 reac _tion_   subtrac _tion_   reflec _tion_

B WORD WORK

Add the same letter to all three words.

1 w a r   s w a m p   s w a n

2 w o l f   w o r r y   w o m a n

3 s a u c e   n i c e l y   j u i c e

4 Write four words that follow the prefix **semi**.

semi- _circle_   semi- _colon_

semi- _detached_   semi- _final_

5 What does **semi** mean? _half_

6 Write four words that follow the prefix **mini**.

mini _bus_   mini _computer_

mini _beast_   mini _cab_

7 What does **mini** mean? _very small_

Write a definition of the word in **bold**.

8 The island was **deserted**.

deserted: _no-one there_

9 There will be a **temporary** bus shelter.

temporary: _there for just a short time_

10 Write an antonym.

deserted   _populated_

temporary   _permanent_

PART B Focus
1–3: spelling patterns
4–7: prefixes; hyphens
8–10: word meanings; antonyms

C SENTENCE WORK

1 Why is an adverb used in this sentence?

Sadly, someone has pulled up some of the plants in the new garden.

To show that the writer thinks this is a sad thing to have happened.

PART C Focus
1–4: adverbs for emphasis; point of view
5–7: figurative and expressive language
8–10: revision of punctuation

Complete these sentences about the same incident.

2 Fortunately, _most of the plants have survived._

3 Unfortunately, _we will need to replant one area._

4 Clearly, _we will have to make the garden more secure._

Complete the sentence.

5 The flowers began to open as if _they were just waking up._

6 The three butterflies fluttered around as if _they were dancing._

7 Rain pounded on the roof as if _we were under attack._

Add the missing punctuation and capital letters.

8 I heard my father's voice. "It's too late," he said.

9 I saw Molly's glove on the floor. Where was she now? Perhaps I could still catch her.

10 "Hello," croaked the frog. "I believe that's my lily pad."

X DEFINITIVE ANSWER   X SAMPLE ANSWER

39

Section 3 Test 9

A WARM-UP

Continue the sentence to make the meaning clear.

1 Put a full stop at the end of a sentence

unless _it is a question or exclamation._

2 Use an apostrophe when _you write the_

shortened form of a word.

3 A dictionary can be used to check a

spelling or _find the meaning of a word._

Add the same two letters to all three words.

4 _au_ t u m n   s _au_ s a g e   b e c _au_ s e

5 c _al_ m   h _al_ v e s   c _al_ v e s

6 l e _ss_ o n   m a _ss_ i v e   p o _ss_ i b l e

Change the prefix to make a different word.

7 ad**just**   _unjust_

8 ad**vent**   _invent_

9 mis**place**   _replace_

10 tele**scope**   _microscope_

> **PART A Focus**
> **1–3:** using conjunctions to clarify meaning
> **4–6:** spelling patterns
> **7–10:** prefixes; word structure

B WORD WORK

Add the correct suffix.

> **PART B Focus**
> **1–6:** adding suffixes; using spelling rules
> **7–10:** giving word meanings

ive ist

1 **decorate** + _ive_ = _decorative_

2 **extreme** + _ist_ = _extremist_

3 **relate** + _ive_ = _relative_

4 **style** + _ist_ = _stylist_

5 What spelling rule did you use?

Drop the final 'e' to add a vowel suffix.

6 Make four words by adding these prefixes and suffixes to the word **use**.

re un able ed less

reuse   _usable_   _unused_   _useless_

7 Add the word to the correct phrase.

energetic thunderous temptation

thunderous applause   a real _temptation_

energetic   dancing

Write a definition.

8 energetic: _lively, with energy_

9 thunderous: _deafening, very loud_

10 temptation: _being tempted_

C SENTENCE WORK

Change the statement into a command.

1 We should stop polluting the Earth.   _Stop polluting the Earth._

2 You could test drive the new ZT.   _Test drive the new ZT._

3 You might like to visit Oakley Gardens.   _Visit Oakley Gardens._

4 Rather than driving to school, you could try walking.   _Don't drive to school. Walk._

Rewrite the sentence, improving the choice of verbs.

5 Marie ran off, her heart beating as she got away.

Marie fled, her heart thumping as she made her escape.

6 The beast came out from its cave, looked around and went back in.

The beast emerged from its cave, glanced around and slid back in.

Add the missing comma.

7 By climbing over the fence, he was able to get a better view.

8 The car suddenly swerved, causing other drivers to brake.

9 Despite the great weather, our holiday was ruined.

10 Why are the commas needed?   _To separate the parts of the sentence._

> **PART C Focus**
> **1–4:** turning statements into commands
> **5–6:** words chosen for effect
> **7–10:** using commas to mark clauses

X DEFINITIVE ANSWER   X SAMPLE ANSWER

Section 3 Test 10

A WARM-UP

Write a sentence using the words in **bold**.

1 **dog curiously**

The dog sniffed curiously at the bone.

2 **acrobat awkwardly**

The acrobat fell awkwardly in the net.

3 **King nervously**

The man spoke nervously to the King.

4 Add the missing letters.

> PART A Focus
> 1–3: sentences with adverbs
> 4–6: spelling strategies
> 7–10: common roots

w _o_ r l d   w _a_ t e r

t _o_ w _a_ r d s   s w _a_ l l _o_ w

Make these words into two-syllable words.

5 cap _ture_   cap _tive_   cap _tain_

6 can _dle_   can _not_   can _cel_

These words and suffixes are mixed up.
Write them correctly.

microscript **auto**vision tele**matic** manu**scope**

7 _microscope_   **9** _automatic_

8 _television_   **10** _manuscript_

B WORD WORK

1 Add a word after the hyphen.

pop- _up_   top- _heavy_   upside- _down_

Cross out the words in **bold** that are wrong for the sentence. Underline the correct spelling.

> PART B Focus
> 1: hyphens
> 2–5: spelling homophones
> 6: spelling rules for adding **able**
> 7–10: word structure and meaning

2 That was ~~grate grait~~ <u>great</u>.

3 We went on a <u>plane</u> ~~plain playn~~.

4 That's what I ~~herd hurd~~ <u>heard</u>.

5 Take a ~~brake~~ <u>break</u> ~~braik~~.

6 Add the suffix **able**.

rely _reliable_   **forgive** _forgivable_

enjoy _enjoyable_   **respect** _respectable_

Add a suffix to the word **protect** or **correct** so that it makes sense in the sentence. Write the word.

tion ly ive

7 I needed _protection_ from my enemies.

8 You guessed the number _correctly_ .

9 They wore _protective_ clothing.

10 There was a _correction_ to be made.

C SENTENCE WORK

Change the nouns into plurals.

1 the **boy's scarf**   *the boys' scarves*

2 the **pirate's patch**   *the pirates' patches*

3 the **child's sandwich**   *the children's sandwiches*

4 the **man's desk**   *the men's desks*

> PART C Focus
> 1–4: apostrophes for possession; plurals
> 5–7: adding clauses to expand and clarify
> 8–10: varying language choice

Continue the sentence to make the point clear.

5 The litter problem will continue unless *we have more bins.*

6 There are some bins, although *they are often full.*

7 The litter is blown around, which *makes it difficult to collect.*

Cross out the word **good** and write a better word. Do not use the same word twice.

8 This is a ~~good~~ bike, which looks ~~good~~ and gives a ~~good~~ ride.   *brilliant   fantastic   superb*

9 This is a ~~good~~ film, with a ~~good~~ cast and ~~good~~ special effects.   *great   wonderful   thrilling*

10 Having a ~~good~~ time. Hotel ~~good~~, food ~~good~~, weather ~~good~~.

lovely   excellent   delicious   fine

Section 3   Test 11

A **WARM-UP**

Is the statement a fact or an opinion?

1 The Earth is round.   _fact_

2 Everyone loves flying.   _opinion_

3 Aeroplanes make the world
   a better place.   _opinion_

4 Aeroplanes use fuel.   _fact_

Add the same short word to complete the three longer words.

5 p o l _ice_   n o t _ice_   s p _ice_

6 l _ear_ n   w _ear_ y   d _ear_

Add a short word to complete the longer word.

7 a t _tent_ i o n

8 i n _vest_ i g a t e

PART A Focus
1–4: fact and opinion
5–8: spelling strategies
9–10: using adverbs

Continue the sentence.

9 Gradually, _the sky began to clear._

10 Surprisingly, _it was not too cold._

B **WORD WORK**

Sort the words into two groups.

fall channel hill label normal pull

1 **one syllable:** _fall_   _hill_   _pull_

2 **two syllables:** _channel_ _label_ _normal_

3 All the one-syllable words end in _double 'l'._

4 Underline the correct spelling.
   normally normaly normalley

5 What spelling rule did you use?
   Add the suffix 'ly' to the root word.

6 Underline the correct spelling.
   traveling **travelling** travelin

PART B Focus
1–7: spelling rules
and conventions;
double letters
8–9: word structure
10: synonyms; word
meanings

7 What spelling rule did you use?
   Double the last letter to add 'ing'.

Remove all prefixes and suffixes. Write the root word.

8 **unsurprisingly** – _un_ _ing_ _ly_ = _surprise_

9 **disheartening** – _dis_ _en_ _ing_ = _heart_

10 Draw a line to join the synonyms.

valiant ———————— inquisitive

boisterous ——————— courageous

curious ———————— lively

C **SENTENCE WORK**

Use some of the words in the statement to make a question for an advertisement.

1 You have to be brave to try this ride.   _Are you brave enough to try?_

2 This is great if you like chocolate.   _Do you like chocolate?_

3 You could win a million pounds.   _Want to win a million?_

4 Complete this haiku about a field of sunflowers.

   Bright yellow faces,   (*5 syllables*)

   Slowly turn towards the sun,   (*7 syllables*)

   Lighting the landscape.   (*5 syllables*)

5 Complete this descriptive sentence.

   The sky was heavy _and a veil of rain fell through the misty air._

PART C Focus
1–3: forming questions
4–5: descriptive language;
extended sentences
6–10: more complex
punctuation

Write the name of the punctuation mark that separates the ideas.

comma dash hyphen semi-colon

6 Save our planet – NOW!   _dash_

7 By turning off the tv, we save energy.   _comma_

8 I was late; the bus had gone.   _semi-colon_

Complete the sentence.

9 He had gone – _completely vanished!_

10 Everything seemed fine – _but it wasn't._

X **DEFINITIVE ANSWER**   X **SAMPLE ANSWER**

Section 3   Test 12

A   WARM-UP

Continue the sentence.

1 Carly fell silent, _thinking about what_
might happen.

2 Marcus peeped out of the door,
hoping no-one would see him.

3 Strangely, _everywhere was silent._

Write two words based on the root word.

4 **hero**   _heroic_   _heroism_

5 **invent**   _inventor_   _invention_

6 **note**   _notice_   _notify_

7 Underline the word that is **not** a verb.

farming <u>seedling</u> watering planting

Put the letters in order to make a word.

8 **a n t u**   _a u n t_

9 **e o r t u**   _r o u t e_

10 **a e l u v**   _v a l u e_

> **PART A Focus**
> **1–3:** extending sentences
> **4–6:** root words
> **7:** word classes
> **8–10:** visual spelling strategies

B   WORD WORK

What do these phrases mean?

1 **he's in hot water**   _he's in trouble_

2 **he cried his eyes out** _he cried a lot_

3 **keep your hair on**   _stay calm_

4 **give me a hand**   _help me_

5 What do you notice about all these phrases?
They are sayings (idioms) and so their
meaning isn't exactly as it seems.

6 Make these adjectives into adverbs.
royal _ly_   lazy _ily_   sure _ly_

7 Make these nouns into adjectives.
accident _al_   mystery _ious_

8 Make these verbs into nouns.
punish _ment_   appear _ance_

> **PART B Focus**
> **1–5:** figures of speech
> **6–8:** word classes;
> spelling rules for
> adding suffixes
> **9–10:** homophones

Cross out the words that are wrong.
Write the correct words.

9 ~~Too~~ bowls of porridge was ~~to~~ much for me
~~two~~ eat.   _Two_   _too_   _to_

10 You can ~~sea there~~ house ~~threw~~ the ~~whole~~
in the fence.
see   _their_   _through_   _hole_

C   SENTENCE WORK

1 Underline the two words or phrases that could be used to introduce a different opinion.

<u>however,</u> moreover, this means, also, <u>on the other hand,</u> finally

Complete the next sentence.

2 The holiday is expensive. However, _it will be worth it._

3 The holiday is expensive. Also, _we need spending money when we get there._

4 The holiday is expensive. This means _that we will have to save up for it._

Add a suitable adverb to show that the writer is not happy.

5 _Unfortunately_ , there was no choice.

6 _Surely_ , this is not correct.

7 _Clearly_ , I will be writing to complain.

> **PART C Focus**
> **1–4:** connectives to link ideas
> **5–7:** adverbs to show point of view
> **8–10:** commas, dash, colon

Continue the sentence. Use a comma, dash or colon before you write the next words.

8 Everything went well _– I think._

9 To make an electrical circuit you need the following _: wires, a battery and a light bulb._

10 Stella jumped in the puddle _, splashing everyone._

Remind the pupil to complete Section 3 of the Progress chart on page 46 of the workbook.   43

Schofield & Sims English Skills 3

Section 3 Writing task assessment sheet: Advert for a new car

Name		Class/Set
Teacher's name		Date

Sentence structure and punctuation

	Always/often	Sometimes	Never
Extends some sentences to clarify meaning (e.g., with explanatory clauses, subordinating connectives)			
Uses adverbs/phrases/clauses to emphasise/persuade			
Uses various types of sentence (e.g., exclamation, question, order, short sentence for impact)			
Varies sentence openings			
Uses person/tense correctly (e.g., **it has**; **you had**)			
Demarcates sentences accurately			
Uses commas to mark phrases and clauses			
Uses possessive apostrophe correctly			
Uses other punctuation (e.g., dashes)			

Composition and effect

Has a clear sense of purpose to engage with/appeal to the reader			
Different sections are indicated by layout			
Ideas developed logically (e.g., main idea, then detail)			
Makes connections between ideas			
Chooses language for effect (e.g., humour, persuasion)			
Uses expanded noun phrases, adjectives, superlatives			
Chooses powerful verbs for impact			
Uses appropriate tone (e.g., friendly)			

Spelling

Phonically regular words spelt correctly			
Applies rules for double/single consonants			
Common letter strings are correct			
Tricky high-/medium-frequency words spelt correctly			
Applies rules for adding prefixes/suffixes			
Applies rules for adding verb endings			
Applies rules for spelling plurals			
Apostrophe used in contracted forms			
Common homophones used correctly			

Writing task summary

From: *English Skills 3 Answers* by Carol Matchett (ISBN 978 07217 1183 6). Copyright © Schofield & Sims Ltd, 2011. Published by Schofield & Sims Ltd, Dogley Mill, Fenay Bridge, Huddersfield HD8 0NQ, UK (www.schofieldandsims.co.uk). **This page may be photocopied for use within your school or institution only.**

Schofield & Sims English Skills 3

Section 3 Completed proofreading task: Our very own kingdom

Name	Class/Set
Teacher's name	Date

It was just a short wark from the carravan. to the beech. We stoped at the
top of the dunes, and looked acros the desertid sand's. It felt like the hole
plaice belongd to us, it was our speshul plaice, as if we was the very furst
peeple to disscover it.

A suden breeze whiped acros the dunes, sending up a flury of sand like a
mini sandstorm, it stinged our legs and arms but we took no notise, it was
just so wunderfull. We beegan runing and showting, tumbleing and stumbleing
down the dunes. our feets keeped sinking into the sand and we was laffing
and shoting to our selfs with hapines, and excitmunt.

Up close, the see was grey and ruff, the waves thundurd onto the sand with
a dangerus roar, it was perfectley gloryus!

Proofreading task summary

Section 3 tasks summary

From: **English Skills 3 Answers** by Carol Matchett (ISBN 978 07217 1183 6). Copyright © Schofield & Sims Ltd, 2011. Published by Schofield & Sims Ltd, Dogley Mill, Fenay Bridge, Huddersfield HD8 0NQ, UK (www.schofieldandsims.co.uk). **This page may be photocopied for use within your school or institution only.**

Full list of the Schofield & Sims English Skills books

Workbooks

For Key Stage 2:

English Skills 1	978 07217 1175 1
English Skills 2	978 07217 1176 8
English Skills 3	978 07217 1177 5
English Skills 4	978 07217 1178 2
English Skills 5	978 07217 1179 9
English Skills 6	978 07217 1180 5

The same workbooks, with covers designed for older users – at Key Stage 3 and beyond:

Essential English Skills 1	978 07217 1188 1
Essential English Skills 2	978 07217 1189 8
Essential English Skills 3	978 07217 1190 4
Essential English Skills 4	978 07217 1191 1
Essential English Skills 5	978 07217 1192 8
Essential English Skills 6	978 07217 1193 5

Answers

Suitable for use with both **English Skills** and **Essential English Skills**:

English Skills 1 Answers	978 07217 1181 2
English Skills 2 Answers	978 07217 1182 9
English Skills 3 Answers	978 07217 1183 6
English Skills 4 Answers	978 07217 1184 3
English Skills 5 Answers	978 07217 1185 0
English Skills 6 Answers	978 07217 1186 7

Teacher's Guide

The **Teacher's Guide** contains the **Workbook descriptors**, **Entry test** and many other useful items suitable for use with both **English Skills** and **Essential English Skills**:

| English Skills Teacher's Guide | 978 07217 1187 4 |

Also available

Mental Arithmetic (for Key Stage 2) and **Essential Mental Arithmetic** (for Key Stage 3 and beyond) are similar in format to **English Skills** and **Essential English Skills**, providing intensive maths practice.

 For further information about both series, and for details of the **I can do** teaching method, which can be used with all the books mentioned on this page, visit **www.schofieldandsims.co.uk**